The Rules in Practice

Sixth Edition

Bryan Willis

fernhurst BOOKS

www.fernhurstbooks.co.uk

Copyright © Bryan Willis 2005

First published 2005 by
Fernhurst Books,
Duke's Path, High Street, Arundel,
West Sussex, BN18 9AJ, UK

Earlier editions published in 1985, 1989, 1993,
1997 and 2001

British Library Cataloguing in Publication Data.
A catalogue record for this book is available
from the British Library.

ISBN 1 904475 14 0

This sixth edition has been updated to comply
with the new rules, which become effective on
1 January 2005.

Printed in China through World Print

Artwork by Creative Byte

Cover design by Simon Balley

Cover photo by Peter Bentley

Drawings from photos by Shelley Baxter

Edited by Tim Davison

The Racing Rules of Sailing are published
courtesy of ISAF (UK) Ltd., Southampton, UK.
© International Sailing Federation, (IOM) Ltd.
June 2004.

**For a free, full-colour brochure
write, phone, fax or email us:**

Fernhurst Books, Duke's Path,
High Street, Arundel, West Sussex
BN18 9AJ, Great Britain.

Phone:	01903 882277
Fax:	01903 882715
Email:	sales@fernhurstbooks.co.uk
Website:	www.fernhurstbooks.co.uk

Contents

The Racing Rules of Sailing for 2005 - 2008

Appendices

Introduction

This book is primarily for competitive sailors who race in dinghies and keelboats. The Racing Rules of Sailing apply to all forms of sailboat racing, though there are some variations for sailboards, match racing, team racing, radio controlled boat racing, etc. I have aimed to examine about one hundred situations that are a regular feature of both championship and club racing. Unlike most other books on the racing rules, I look at these situations from the point of view of you, the helmsman. Placing you in each of the boats involved in turn, I explain your rights and your obligations. Being confident about this knowledge not only means you avoid breaking a rule and have to take a penalty, but that you can concentrate on exploiting the situation to gain boat lengths over your immediate rivals.

It is popular misconception that to be good at boat-to-boat tactics you need to know the rules. The rules, the rule numbers, the case law - all that can be sorted out before the start of the hearing if there is a protest. What you need to know out there on the water are your rights and your obligations; what you are allowed to do, and what you must and mustn't do. You need to know them automatically and subconsciously, so that you can concentrate on manoeuvring and sailing fast, to exploit the situation to the full. It is just as satisfying to come away from a mark in the lead having approached it in second place as it is to spend twenty minutes overhauling your rival with superior boatspeed. Conversely, there is no satisfaction in sailing faster than everyone else on a leg if you throw away your position through being uncertain about your rights and obligations when you come to round the mark.

The book should also be useful in the preparation of a protest, or the defence should you be protested. Each situation shows the critical questions which have to be considered and which will determine the 'facts found' and, therefore, the result of the hearing.

Because almost all the rules of racing apply to the boats rather than to the people sailing them, most books on the rules, and indeed the rules themselves, use the pronoun 'she'. Since I aim to look at situations from the point of view of you, the helmsman, I use the pronoun 'you'; and for the helmsman of the other boat 'he' and 'him'*. However, bear in mind that it is what the boat does that matters. The intentions of the people sailing the boats are irrelevant (provided that they are not malicious). Even most hails are irrelevant. What each boat actually does is usually all that counts.

This sixth edition has been updated to comply with the changes that come into force on 1st January 2005 published by the ISAF (the International Sailing Federation).

* *Publisher's note: or 'she' is implied throughout.*

The Rule Changes

Every four years the rules are updated. In 1997 there was a major revision of rules and terminology. The old 'Yacht Racing Rules' became the new simplified 'Racing Rules of Sailing'. A leeward boat was no longer allowed to 'luff as she pleased' and everyone became required to try to avoid collisions. Since 1997 there have been numerous small changes, mostly for clarification, and the most significant of these are included in this section.

For most sailors, none of the changes are significant and will not affect the way they sail. But to some sailors, and some race committees, some will be important. The best plan is to scan through all the changes and mark those that you think are relevant to you. All changes have been incorporated into the book. If you are new to racing, it is best not to read these changes: who cares how the situation has changed? Get straight into the book!

- The standard penalty for breaking a 'when boats meet' rule (which is the penalty that applies unless the sailing instructions say otherwise) is still the '720'. However, it has been renamed and reworded to reflect a change. It is now called the Two-Turns Penalty, and provided the two turns are done in the same direction and contain two tacks and two gybes, if it's short of 720 degrees that no longer matters.

- The un-numbered rule 'SPORTSMANSHIP AND THE RULES' is given better prominence to emphasize its importance. A small change of wording has been made to make it clear that when a boat retires after breaking a rule of Part 2 (the 'when boats meet' rules), she cannot be disqualified in a hearing for the same breach. (There have been a significant number of protest committees that have disqualified boats in a hearing even though they retired in recognition of breaking a rule in the same incident.)

- A boat sailing under the racing rules that meets a boat that is not, must comply with the Collision Regulations. A boat can no longer protest another boat for breaking the Colregs. Only the Race Committee or the Protest Committee can protest.

- Organizers of ocean races often require boats to switch to the Collision Regulations at night. It is now clear that it is the rules of Part 2 (when boats meet) which are replaced by the right-of-way rules of the Collision Regulations or by government right-of-way rules.

- When two boats are tacking at the same time, and one is clear astern of the other, neither of the boats was required to keep clear of the other. Now the boat clear astern must keep clear.

- The 'room at marks and obstructions' rule doesn't apply at a windward mark. That hasn't changed, but there was a problem at a leeward mark when boats were tacking onto a proper course after rounding. New wording (actually the wording from the 1997-2000 rules) is intended to resolve the problem so that sailors can be sure that at every mark other than a windward mark, the 'room at marks and obstructions' rule applies. For example, if the course from the leeward mark to the finish means you need to tack immediately to sail for the finish line, the outside boat must give you room to do so, if you had the right to room coming into the mark.

- Rule 18.2(c) (regarding the rights and obligations of boats when one is clear ahead of the other as they reach the Two-Length Zone) has been changed slightly to clarify that if the boat that was clear ahead tacks, then the obligation on the boat that was clear astern to keep clear, and give room if she becomes overlapped on the outside, is removed.

- A right-of-way boat that changes course must normally give room to a keep-clear boat to keep clear. When changing course to round or pass a mark, however, she does not have that obligation. This has not changed. What has changed is that she is relieved of this obligation only after the starting signal. This will be important as boats approach and pass the back of the committee boat.

- When beating to windward a boat needing to tack because of an obstruction (such as the shore) can hail for room to a boat astern or to windward. Nothing new about that. But there was a flaw in the rule that meant if the boat needing room was above close-hauled she didn't have the right to hail; an awkward situation for a boat that had luffed above close-hauled before she realised she needed room to tack. This has been resolved so that the boat may be 'close-hauled or above'. There is a new clause to clarify that to hail for room to tack when in fact there is no safety issue, breaks the rule.

- There is now a requirement for a boat not to interfere with another boat that is on another leg of the course or, where the course is several laps, on another lap. This is to prevent a boat, that can discard her final race results and needs to prevent her rival finishing in a top position, from skipping a mark. The new wording is not aimed at stopping the tactics of Ben Ainslie in the final Laser race of the 2000 Sydney Olympics (which is still a legitimate tactic), but if the rival slips past, it will prevent skipping a mark and manoeuvring against the rival on the next leg. This rule has been in the Match and Team racing appendices, but now it applies to all disciplines.

- The definitions of a 'party' have been extended to include the 'organising authority', so it is clearer that a boat may seek redress from the protest committee because of an error or omission of the organising authority (in addition to the race committee).

- A national authority (e.g. the Royal Yachting Association, United States Sailing Association, Australian Yachting Federation), in its 'Prescriptions to the Rules', may now limit the rules permitted to be changed by sailing instructions.

- The definition describing how a boat 'starts' has been revised to clarify that before a boat can start she has to be entirely on the pre-course side of the line, and having complied with the requirements of the 'round-the-ends' rule (if it is in force and the boat was over the line in the final minute).

- There is a requirement for an Organising Authority to make the Notice of Race (in addition to the sailing instructions) available to boats.

- The rule that requires a boat to 'sail the course' has been changed so that a boat that crosses the finishing line can nevertheless go back and correct an error in sailing the course, and a boat doesn't finish in a multi-lap course as she sails through the finishing line on each lap, until she has completed the course.

- When the 'black flag rule' is in force for a start, and a boat breaks the rule (by being on the course side during the final minute), and there is a general recall or the race is abandoned, the race committee (at the start line) is now required to display the boat's sail number (in the starting area) before the next warning signal. No signal will be given when a boat or boats are on the course side at the starting signal.

- The provision for an 'S' flag to be displayed on a committee boat before the start to signify that a shortened course is to be sailed, has been removed. The meaning of the 'S flag' displayed from the committee boat at the finishing line is now specified in the rules so that it is unnecessary to specify in the sailing instructions: 'between a rounding mark and the committee boat, a line through which boats are required to pass at the end of each lap, or between two gate marks'. The race committee may shorten course so that other scheduled races can be sailed.

- The rule describing how a race committee changes a course by signalling at a rounding mark at the beginning of the changed leg, has been revised. The mark at the end of the changed leg need not be in position at the time the change is signalled (this avoids a sailing instruction to this effect). A new signal (green or red triangular flag) is included as an alternative to 'the new compass bearing' being displayed.

- When a mark goes missing or drifts significantly out of position, the race committee may replace it with a mark of similar appearance or, alternatively, with an object displaying flag M, and make repetitive sound signals.

- As from 1st January 2006, trapeze and hiking harnesses must have a device that can release the competitor from the boat quickly at any time while in use.

- The 'outside help' rule has been extensively revised to make clear what outside help is permitted: help when persons or vessel are in danger, help for an ill or injured crew member, help from the crew of the other boat to get clear after a collision; help in the form of information freely available to all boats, and unsolicited information from a disinterested source, which may be another boat in the same race.

- Some of the 'prohibited actions' in the 'Propulsion' rule have been modified slightly: 'repeated fanning of any sail either by pulling in (was 'trimming') and releasing the sail' and 'repeated rolling of the boat, induced by body movement or by repeated (new adjective) adjustment of the sails or centreboard, or by steering (new)', and sculling has been changed to: 'repeated movement of the helm that is either forceful or that propels the boat forward or prevents her from moving astern (was 'repeated movement of the helm not necessary for steering').

- There are some additions to the 'exceptions' (in other words, these actions are now permitted): 'A boat may be rolled to facilitate steering', 'When a boat is above a close-hauled course and either stationary or moving slowly, she may scull to turn to a close-hauled course' and 'A boat may reduce speed by repeatedly moving her helm'.

- When there is damage or injury that is obvious to the boats involved the requirement for a protest flag for boats over 6 metres is removed. This will avoid protests being found to be invalid for technical reasons when there is damage or injury. It continues to be the case that boats under 6 metres are not required by the rules to display a protest flag.

- There is clarification as to when a protest committee may and may not protest a boat. It can't protest based on information from an interested party, or an invalid protest (unless there may have been injury or serious damage). If the protest committee is hearing a valid protest and suspects a third party is to blame, it must adjourn the hearing, inform the third party that the protest committee is protesting her, and then hold the new and adjourned hearings together.

- A protest may be lodged with only a description of the incident provided that the identity of the protestee is established before the hearing.

- It is clearer that a boat may request redress not only if the boat itself is physically damaged but also if a person is injured, when the other boat broke a rule of Part 2 ('When boats meet').

- There were always arguments as to which rule applied when there was a conflict between a Sailing Instruction and a rule in the Notice of Race. There is a new rule that requires the Protest Committee to '... apply the rule that it believes will provide the fairest result for all boats affected'.

- It is made clear that a protest committee may act on a report from any source when considering opening a 'gross misconduct' hearing. When a competitor has left the venue, the committee must not hold a hearing but may submit a report to the competitor's national authority.

There has always been a restriction on which bodies can change which rules. National authorities and, more importantly, organising authorities, are no longer permitted to change rule 42 (Propulsion) but there is still no restriction on a class organisation changing rule 42 in their class rules. However, it continues to be the case that national authorities may prescribe that rules may be changed 'to develop or test proposed rules'.

- ISAF (the International Sailing Federation) itself may authorise changes to any Racing Rule in exceptional circumstances for a specific international event (such as the America's Cup).

- A national authority may now restrict changes to its prescriptions, so that organising authorities cannot simply write a sailing instruction to say the national prescriptions don't apply.

- The 'notice of race' may be changed if 'adequate notice is given'.

- Gone is the confusing term 'jury' (without the adjective 'international'). Whether appointed by the organising authority or the race committee, the body will be known as a 'protest committee'. (At major international events, the organising authority will still appoint an 'international jury'.)

- Sailing instructions used to have to state the scoring system to be used for an event. Now, if it's not mentioned it is, by default, the commonly used 'Low Point' scoring system (first gets 1 point, second gets 2 points etc.).

If only the leading boat finishes within the time limit (validating the race for the other boats), but then retires, it was argued that the race should not be scored. It is now clear that it will be.

1 The Basics

There are certain obligations that you have all the time, so I will state them here and not repeat them in the rest of the book.

You must sail fairly. Sailboat racing is the greatest sport. Generally, we don't have umpires or judges or referees; we police ourselves. Cheats can spoil any sport, and currently our sport is almost free of cheats (unlike some other sports). We all need to work to keep it that way. So the rules require that as a sailor you conduct yourself in a sportsmanlike manner at all times, and don't bring the sport into disrepute. This principle applies as much to club racing as it does to championships. Trying to gain an advantage by deliberately infringing a rule or lying at a protest hearing is cheating and the penalties for cheating can be severe. In recent years, competitors found guilty of cheating have been disqualified from entire championships and some have been banned by their national authorities or by the International Sailing Federation from taking part in competitive sailing for a year or more (Basic Principle: 'Sportsmanship and the Rules' & Rule 69 'Allegations of Gross Misconduct').

You must help anyone you see in danger. If you lose a position while acting the hero, you will be entitled to redress. (Rule 1 'Helping those in danger', Rule 60.1(b) 'Right to ... Request Redress', Rule 62.1(c) 'Redress').

When you break a rule of Part 2 ('When Boats Meet'), and the other party is clearly aggrieved, you must promptly do your penalty turns. To continue to race without taking a penalty knowing you have broken a rule, hoping perhaps that no one will protest, or through your courtroom skills you might outwit a protestor in the protest room, is an infringement of the Basic Principle 'Sportsmanship and the Rules'.

Even when you have right-of-way or the right to room, you must try to avoid contact. If you don't, and there is damage, you must take a penalty. If there is serious damage, then the alternative penalty option is not open to you and you must retire. (Rule 14 'Avoiding Contact', Rule 44.1 'Taking a Penalty').

Whether or not you may display advertising on your hull or sails will usually depend on what your class association has decided at an AGM. If you go to an open regatta, the organisers might require you to put advertising (which they will supply) on the forward part of your hull. You may advertise (if it's not offensive) as much as you like on clothing. (Rule 79 'Advertising' and the ISAF Advertising Code).

I emphasise that these principles apply all the time, and to every situation described in this book.

If you are involved in an incident during a race and you believe another boat (or boats) broke a rule, and you want to protest if he doesn't take a penalty, then you must hail 'protest' at the first reasonable opportunity. In addition, if your hull is 6 metres long or more, you need to display a protest flag and keep it displayed until the end of the race.

There are a few terms and definitions that you need to know before we start. (See also page 127.)

International Sailing Federation (ISAF)

The international governing body that publishes the racing rules and, for guidance on their interpretation, publishes cases that have been decided and submitted by national authorities. (The A in ISAF is there because the International Softball Federation seized the initials ISF before the ISAF changed its name in September 1996 from the International Yacht Racing Union.)

National Authority

Every sailing nation has a national body to administer sailing on waters within its jurisdiction. In Great Britain this is the Royal Yachting Association, in the United States it is the US Sailing Association, in Australia the Australian Yachting Federation, in New Zealand Yachting New Zealand, and so on.

Organising Authority

The body that decides to hold an event and arranges the venue. The organising authority might be a club, a class association or a national authority, or a combination of these. At least one of its constituents must be affiliated to the national authority. Sailing clubs are Organising Authorities for their club racing. They might be affiliated to their national authorities through state or district organisations that are in turn affiliated to the national authority. An international class association usually joins with a club to form the Organising Authority to run a world championship. The Organising Authority must appoint a race committee. At a principal event (such as an open regatta or a national championship) it may also appoint a protest committee, or at an international event, an international jury.

Race committee

The race committee, appointed by the Organising Authority, is responsible for producing sailing instructions, organising the racing and publishing the results. When no jury or international jury has been appointed, the race committee must form or appoint a protest committee when one is needed.

Protest committee

A protest committee is appointed by the organising authority for an event, or on an 'ad hoc' basis by the race committee to hear protests and requests for redress. The term 'protest committee' is sometimes used to describe an international jury when it hears protests and requests for redress. A protest committee may also be required to go afloat during dinghy regattas to encourage rule compliance and implement the 'yellow flag protest system' for penalising boats breaking Rule 42 'Propulsion'.

International jury

Appointed by the organising authority, its membership is made up of people of different nationalities, the majority of whom must be international judges (appointed by the ISAF). Provided that it conducts itself in accordance with the procedures described in Appendix N, its decisions are not open to appeal.

Appeal authority

Each national authority appoints a committee to hear appeals by competitors (and race committees) against decisions of protest committees and juries (but not International Juries). For example, in the United Kingdom, the Royal Yachting Association's Racing Rules Group hears appeals; in the United States of America, appeals are decided by District Appeals Committees, and some are subsequently referred to the United States Sailing Association's Appeals Committee.

There is no higher appeal authority than the one provided by the national authority having jurisdiction over the event. The International Sailing Federation does not hear appeals.

Obstruction

'An obstruction is an object that a boat could not pass without changing course substantially, if she were sailing directly towards it and one of her hull lengths from it. An object that can be safely passed on only one side and an area so designated by the sailing instructions are also obstructions. However, a boat racing is not an obstruction to other boats unless they are required to keep clear of her, give her room or, if Rule 21 applies, avoid her.' The committee boat, a rescue boat, a capsized dinghy, the shore, perceived underwater dangers or shallows, and a boat on starboard-tack on a collision course in relation to a port-tack boat are all obstructions. In the case of the committee boat it will also be a mark when it is specified as being at one end of the starting or finish line. A half-metre diameter inflatable buoy is not an obstruction whether or not it is a mark.

The 'Two-length Zone'

The area around a mark or obstruction within a distance of two hull lengths of the boat nearer to it. The zone is critical to right to room to pass or round a mark or obstruction. It is relevant only to boats approaching or rounding or passing a mark. After boats have left the mark astern, the zone has no more relevance.

Keeping clear (see diagram opposite)

'One boat keeps clear of another if the other can sail her (current straight-line) course with no need to take avoiding action and, when the boats are overlapped on the same tack, if the leeward boat could change course in both directions without immediately making contact with the windward boat.' In dinghies in a Force 2 on flat water, 'keeping clear' can be synonymous with 'avoiding a collision' (for example in a 'port and starboard' encounter on a beat in which the port-tack boat ducks under the stern of the starboard-tack boat), but were they to be large keelboats in a Force 6 and a heavy sea, an obligation on you to 'keep clear' might mean leaving a boat-length or more between you and the right-of-way boat. Further-more, when you are the give-way boat, you must not intimidate the right-of-way boat such that he thinks there is going to be a collision and is forced to take avoiding action. So even in fairly light conditions it's as well to look under the boom and give him a smile, so he knows you are paying attention,

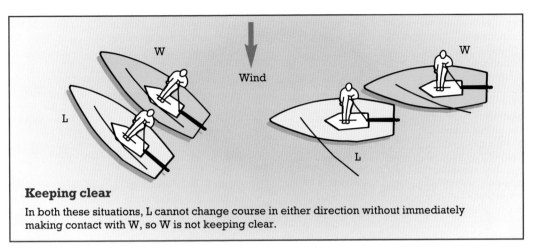

Keeping clear

In both these situations, L cannot change course in either direction without immediately making contact with W, so W is not keeping clear.

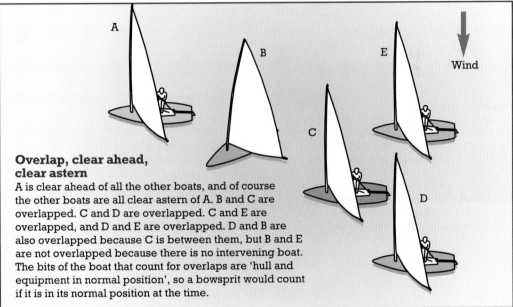

Overlap, clear ahead, clear astern

A is clear ahead of all the other boats, and of course the other boats are all clear astern of A. B and C are overlapped. C and D are overlapped. C and E are overlapped, and D and E are overlapped. D and B are also overlapped because C is between them, but B and E are not overlapped because there is no intervening boat. The bits of the boat that count for overlaps are 'hull and equipment in normal position', so a bowsprit would count if it is in its normal position at the time.

before diving under his stern and missing him by a millimetre.

Hailing

A hail is a meaningful word or string of words capable of being heard in the prevailing conditions by the occupants of the boat to which it is addressed. (This is not a defined term - but it's a useful definition, supported by appeal cases.)

You are never actually **required** to make a hail, but when you want to protest you have to hail 'protest' at the first reasonable opportunity; and

when you're approaching an obstruction close-hauled and need a boat to give you room to tack, he is not required to take any action until you hail.

When the other boat hails you, you don't always have to respond. You should remember the situations when you must respond to a hail from the other boat:

- When he hails for room to tack because he's close-hauled approaching an obstruction.

- When, after you have hailed for room to tack

because you are close-hauled and need room to tack at an obstruction, he replies 'you tack'.

Some other hails might help to establish something, such as the right to room at a mark, or warn a port-tack boat of your presence ('Starboard!') but these hails in themselves place no obligation on anyone to do anything, so they have no real relevance.

When a hail from you means the other boat must respond, there is an obligation on you not to make the hail unless the conditions exist for you to make the hail. For example, when you are close-hauled and believe you are approaching shallow water and cannot tack without the possibility of colliding with a boat astern or to windward, you may of course hail for room to tack, but you have no right to hail merely for tactical reasons.

Layline

The course on which your boat, sailing close-hauled on starboard tack, can just lay a windward mark which is to be rounded to port is the starboard-tack layline for that mark, and the most windward line on which you would approach the mark on port tack is the port-tack layline. High performance boats with powerful asymmetric spinnakers or gennakers go much faster down-wind by reaching and gybing, so a leeward mark has laylines which are the proper courses for the boats approaching on each tack. Tidal streams distort laylines; a stream going with the wind makes the angle between the windward mark port and starboard laylines wider, and the leeward mark laylines narrower. As the wind gets lighter, the angle between the leeward mark laylines for high-performance boats with asymmetric spinnakers or gennakers gets dramatically wider. A cross-course tidal stream swings the laylines towards the tide. 'Layline' is not a term used in the rulebook, but the term 'proper course' is, and laylines are the extremes of proper courses, so need to be understood. And of course an under-standing of laylines is essential for all tacticians.

Luffing rights

This term is not used in the rulebook either, but sailors often use it, and so I use it in this book. You have 'luffing rights' when you have the right to sail higher than your proper course, forcing a boat to windward of you to change course to keep clear. Provided you didn't establish the overlap to leeward of the windward boat, from astern and within two lengths, a leeward boat has luffing

rights, and may luff right up to head-to-wind, but she must give the windward boat room to keep clear. (Rules 11 and 16)

Before the starting signal there is no 'proper course' so any leeward boat may luff up to head-to-wind no matter how the overlap was established (provided the windward boat can keep clear). But at the moment the starting signal is made, any leeward boat that established the overlap from clear astern within two lengths must bear away to close-hauled (if the first leg is a beat) unless as a result of sailing above close-hauled she promptly sails astern of the other boat (which allows her to tack out of the windward boat's windshadow). (Rules 11, 16 and 17.1)

Proper course (see diagram opposite)

A proper course is 'A course a boat would sail to finish as soon as possible in the absence of the other boats referred to in the rule using the term. A boat has no proper course before her starting signal.' You're never required to sail a proper course, but there are some situations in which you mustn't sail above your proper course, and others in which you mustn't sail below your proper course, so you need to know what a proper course is.

Sailing instructions

The race committee must produce sailing instructions and make them available to you in time for you to read them before the race or series. They contain two types of information:

• The intentions of the race committee; these instructions contain the word 'will'. For example, 'All marks will be large orange spheres'.

• The obligations of boats and individual competitors; these instruction contain the word 'shall'. For example, 'All marks shall be rounded to port'.

The two types of instructions are mixed together because they are ordered chronologically.

It is imperative that you read the sailing instructions carefully before a race or series. I doubt if there is a champion who has not at some time lost an important race or series through failing to read or remember some particular sailing instruction.

The penalty for not complying with a sailing instruction describing a boat's obligation is

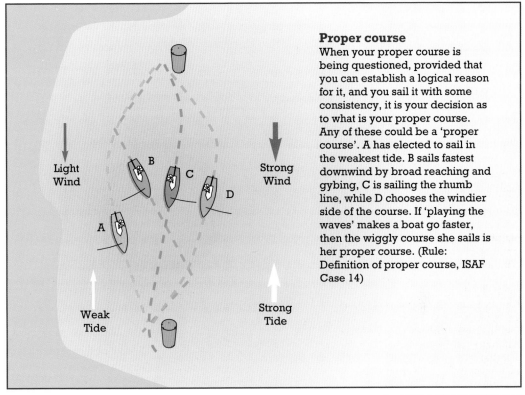

Proper course

When your proper course is being questioned, provided that you can establish a logical reason for it, and you sail it with some consistency, it is your decision as to what is your proper course. Any of these could be a 'proper course'. A has elected to sail in the weakest tide. B sails fastest downwind by broad reaching and gybing, C is sailing the rhumb line, while D chooses the windier side of the course. If 'playing the waves' makes a boat go faster, then the wiggly course she sails is her proper course. (Rule: Definition of proper course, ISAF Case 14)

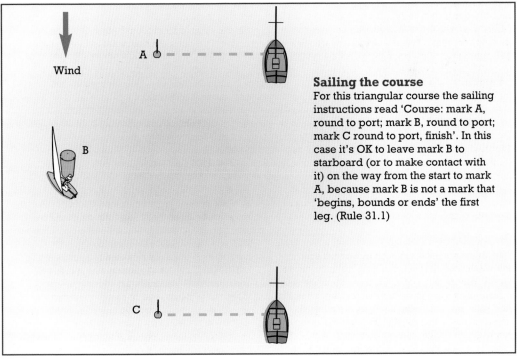

Sailing the course

For this triangular course the sailing instructions read 'Course: mark A, round to port; mark B, round to port; mark C round to port, finish'. In this case it's OK to leave mark B to starboard (or to make contact with it) on the way from the start to mark A, because mark B is not a mark that 'begins, bounds or ends' the first leg. (Rule 31.1)

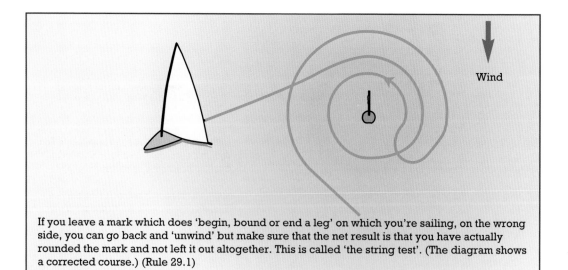

If you leave a mark which does 'begin, bound or end a leg' on which you're sailing, on the wrong side, you can go back and 'unwind' but make sure that the net result is that you have actually rounded the mark and not left it out altogether. This is called 'the string test'. (The diagram shows a corrected course.) (Rule 29.1)

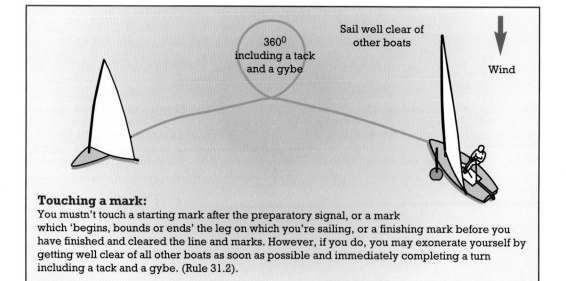

Touching a mark:

You mustn't touch a starting mark after the preparatory signal, or a mark which 'begins, bounds or ends' the leg on which you're sailing, or a finishing mark before you have finished and cleared the line and marks. However, if you do, you may exonerate yourself by getting well clear of all other boats as soon as possible and immediately completing a turn including a tack and a gybe. (Rule 31.2).

disqualification from a race (unless some other penalty is specified), but the penalty can usually be applied only after a hearing.

No such penalty can be applied to the race committee when it does not carry out its own intentions specified in the sailing instructions, or it fails to comply with a rule which governs its conduct (Parts 3 and 7 of the Rules). What penalty could be imposed without adversely affecting innocent competitors? (The committee could be hung, drawn and quartered, but who would run the next race?) You should bear in mind that the race committee is invariably trying to do a good job of running the races. If the committee makes an error or an omission that affects your finishing position in the race or series, and if this is through no fault of your own, then you can ask for 'redress'. A good race committee, realising its erroneous action has affected a boat's finishing position, will itself initiate a redress hearing. Chapter 17 deals with redress hearings. One of the most common errors is to write confusing or ambiguous sailing instructions about the course, resulting in some boats sailing one course and some sailing another.

2 Before the Preparatory Signal

Before going afloat you usually have to enter, register or 'sign on' and may be required to show your boat's measurement certificate. These requirements will be described in the sailing instructions.

To the water! Although the 'when boats meet' rules apply in the same way before as they do after the preparatory signal, there is no penalty for breaking a rule of Part 2 ('when boats meet') unless you interfere with a boat that is racing. (Rule 22.1)

If you break a rule of Part 2 before the preparatory signal, you do not need to retire or take a penalty (but you or your insurance company might have to pay for the damage if there is any).

The rules or sailing instructions (including all of Part 4 of the rules) requiring you to do something 'whilst racing' don't apply before the preparatory signal either, because you're not 'racing' till the preparatory signal.

However, you can be disqualified (after a protest and a hearing) for breaking some other sailing instruction, even if you're not racing when the infringement occurs.

If your boat is damaged in a collision and it wasn't your fault, it is useful to be able to present to your insurance company a protest form showing that the hearing found the other boat to be in the wrong. So it's worth remembering that you can protest another boat for breaking a rule of Part 2 (the 'when boats meet' rules) before the preparatory signal or after the finish, and if the other boat does not accept that he broke a rule, the race committee must hear the protest if it is valid, even though no penalty is applied to the other boat. You must hail 'Protest', and lodge the written protest within the time limit.

The standard signalling system for starting a race is a series of visual signals (usually flags) each accompanied by a sound signal. The sequence begins with the 'Warning Signal' (usually your class flag) at five minutes before the start. One minute later is the 'Preparatory Signal' signalling the beginning of the four-minute 'preparatory period' in which boats are 'racing' (even though they are not going anywhere) and a boat breaking a rule of Part 2 must take an exonerating turns penalty. The visual signal is usually the code flag 'P' (blue with a white square in the middle) which means there will be no 'starting penalty'. At one minute before the start, the preparatory flag is lowered, and at the start the class flag is lowered. When there is a lot of boats all eager to get a good start, the race committee can substitute the 'P' flag with an 'I', a 'Z' or a 'black flag' to bring into effect a penalty system during the final minute. (Rules 26 and 30)

The sailing instructions might vary the standard signalling system. For example, the Warning Signal might be 10 minutes before the start instead of the standard five.

You should be near the committee boat and watching it closely when the Preparatory Signal is made so that you can set your watch. This is especially important in a big fleet where you might start some distance from the committee boat and it is often impossible to see the visual starting signal or hear the 'gun' (and remember the sound takes a while to travel the length of a long starting line).

3 In the Preparatory Period

This section covers the period from the preparatory signal to the time at which boats are approaching the line to start.

At the moment of the preparatory signal your boat must be afloat and off moorings and thereafter not be hauled out or 'made fast' (tied up) except to bail or reef or make repairs. However, you may anchor at any time, but you must recover your anchor if possible before proceeding. Your crew may stand on the bottom (in shallow water of course) to hold the boat. (Rule 45)

You are vulnerable in the preparatory period because no one is sailing any particular course so the risk of collision is great. However, if you break a rule of Part 2 (the 'when boats meet' rules) you can take a penalty (by getting well clear of other boats and doing a 'Two-Turns Penalty' as soon as possible after the incident). So unless the infringement is shortly before the starting signal, the penalty is a light one. (Rule 44.1)

If you hit a starting mark, you may exonerate yourself by getting well clear of other boats as soon as possible and doing a one-turn penalty. (Rule 31.2)

If you are going to sail in championships or open regattas, you need to know the starting penalty signals and systems because they may affect the way you plan your start (balancing the risk of being a premature starter and the reward of getting a cracking good start):

No penalty

The vast majority of races are started with no penalty system in force. The P flag is used as the preparatory signal. You are allowed to be on the course side of the starting line right up to the starting signal. If any part of your boat, crew or equipment is on the wrong side of the line at the moment of the starting signal, you simply have to get back completely behind the line to start properly (known as a 'dip start'). On a starting line with plenty of room, the cost of making a mistake (by crossing prematurely) is small.

The I flag ('Round the ends') penalty system

When an I flag is displayed as the preparatory signal, the 'round the ends' rule will come into effect when the flag is struck at the 'one minute signal' (one minute before the starting signal). This means that in the final minute, if any part of your boat is on the course side of the line, you must return to the pre-start side round one of the ends of the line. The idea of the rule is that it stops boats milling around on the course side of the line in the final minute, and encourages boats not to cross the start line prematurely, especially in the middle of the starting line. (Rule 30.1)

The Z flag (20%) penalty system

When a Z flag is displayed as the preparatory signal, if any part of your boat is on the wrong side of the line in the final minute, your finishing position will have 20% of the number of boats entered for the race added on. If any part of your boat is on the wrong side of the line at the start, you must return to start. If there is a 'general recall', or the race is abandoned and resailed, the 20% penalty is still applied.

The black flag ('disqualification')

When a black flag is displayed with the preparatory signal, and in the final minute any part of your boat is on the wrong side of the line, you will be disqualified, unless the race is postponed or abandoned before the starting signal. If there is a general recall you must not start in the next attempt to get the race under way. Even if the race doesn't get started that day, you won't be eligible to start in it when it does get started.

These 'starting penalty' systems can be brought into force for any start. The race committee simply displays the appropriate flag as the preparatory signal.

Now to the boat-to-boat situations......

You are A:
• You're on port tack (because your sail is on the starboard side) so you're the give-way boat and you must keep clear. (Rule 10)
• If you change course so that you are no longer on a collision course, and B changes course back onto a collision course, you must change course again and make every effort to keep clear. (Rule 10)

You are B:
• You're the right-of-way boat.
• You may change course, but if you do you must give A room to keep clear, so you mustn't change course so close to A as to prevent him from keeping clear. At a protest hearing, if there is a collision and doubt whether in altering course close to A you failed to give him room, a protest committee is likely to find against you. (Rule 16)

B has established an overlap from clear astern.

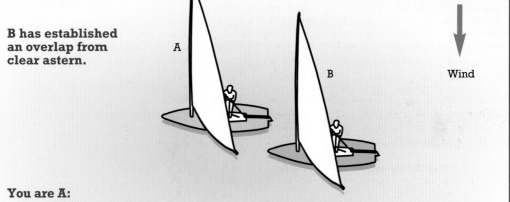

You are A:
• While there's no overlap, you may change course as you please; you have no obligations.
• When B gets his overlap to leeward, the situation changes and you must now keep clear of him.
• You need do nothing till there's an overlap, even if you are sitting 'hove-to'; but once he's established the overlap you must manoeuvre to keep clear (by luffing or drawing ahead or even tacking if need be). Bear in mind once he's given you a chance to keep clear, he's allowed to luff right up to head-to-wind. (Rules 11 & 15)

You are B:
• While you are clear astern you must keep clear. (Rule 12)
• You mustn't establish an overlap so close to A that if A luffed or bore away he would immediately make contact (Rules 11, Definition of 'keep clear')
• Once the boats are overlapped, you become the right-of-way boat and may luff right up to head-to-wind. However, you must give A room to keep clear. Even if you don't luff, you can't come charging in while A is hove-to and not initially give him room to pull his sail in and get going. (Rules 11, 15, 16)

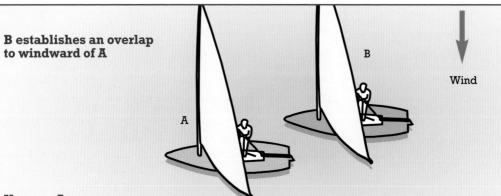

B establishes an overlap to windward of A

You are A:

• Before the overlap you have no obligations, except that any change of course must be such that it gives B room to keep clear. (Rules 12 & 16)

• When B gets an overlap nothing changes; you may still change course if you wish and you must give B room to keep clear. (Rules 11 & 16)

• You may continue to luff, up to head-to-wind, provided you give B room to keep clear. (Rules 11 & 16)

• However, if there is an obstruction (such as the committee boat) to windward of B which prevents B from responding, then you may not luff; indeed you may even have to bear away to give B room to pass the obstruction. (Rules 18.1, 18.2(a))

You are B:

• You must keep clear before and after you are overlapped. (Rules 12 & 11)

The general principle about windward and leeward situations in the preparatory period is that a leeward boat may luff up to head-to-wind provided she gives the windward boat room to keep clear. It doesn't matter how the overlap was established, or the relative positions fore-and-aft of the two boats. The windward boat must keep clear.

A and B are overlapped approaching an obstruction (which may or may not be a mark), before they are approaching the line to start

You are A: You must keep clear, but if B decides to go under the committee boat, you have the right to room if you want to do the same.

You are B: You may choose to go either to windward or to leeward of the committee boat, in spite of any protestations from A. But if you decide to go to windward, you must change course in such a way that A is able to keep clear. If you go to leeward you must give A room to pass under the committee boat if he wants to. (Rules 11, 16 & 18.2(a))

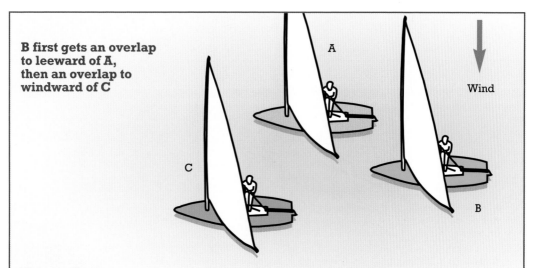

B first gets an overlap to leeward of A, then an overlap to windward of C

Wind

You are A: When B first gets an overlap to leeward of you, because there is a possibility of his bow running into your boom, you must begin to manoeuvre to keep clear. If B luffs after he gets the overlap, you will have to luff too. If B is sailing higher than you are, you'll have to luff, but you don't have to begin to do anything until there is an overlap. (Rule 11)

You are B: When you're astern, you must keep clear. When you first get the overlap to leeward of A, it must not be so close that if A luffs there will immediately be contact. You must give A room to keep clear. Provided you give room, you may luff. You must keep clear of C even if he luffs. If there is not enough room between A and C for you to get between them when you first get your overlap to windward of C, then you don't have the right to go in there. C has the right to luff, and if he chooses to luff the gap will get smaller, so you'll be in a pretty precarious position! (Rules 12, 11, 18.5 & Definition of 'Keep Clear')

You are C: You may luff if you wish, but if you do you must allow B and A room to keep clear. (Rule 16)

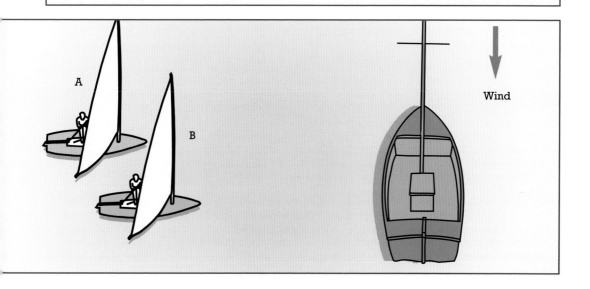

Wind

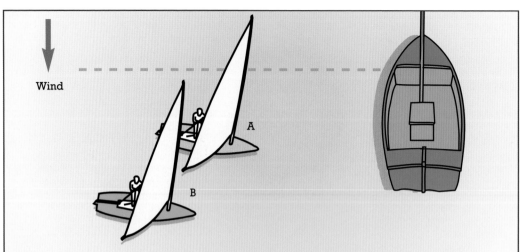

You are A: You have the right to room to pass under the committee boat even though it's a starting mark because you are not 'approaching the line to start'. You don't have to hail, but it's probably a good idea if you think you're not being given enough room. You can change your mind and tack if you want to.

You are B: It is too late now to decide to go to windward of the committee boat, so you must give room to A whether he asks for it or not. You need to give sufficient room for A to pass 'in a seamanlike way'. (Rule 18.2(a))

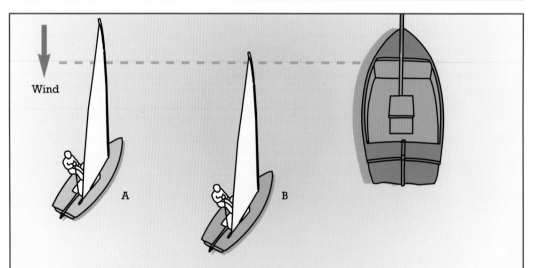

You are A: You are the give-way boat and if B luffs you must keep clear, but if B tacks you become the right-of-way boat while he's tacking and B must keep clear of you. (Rules 11 & 13)

You are B: You have no right to hail for room to tack (whether or not you are approaching the starting line to start) because the committee boat is a starting mark and the rules don't give you the right to room to tack at a starting mark if it's surrounded by navigable water. You had better bear away before you get trapped. If there are any boats to leeward of you they must give you room to pass under the committee boat. (Rule 19.2 & 18.2(a))

4 The Start

This section covers the period from your approach to the starting line shortly before the starting signal, to when you have started and cleared the starting line.

The race committee must make the time between the preparatory signal and the starting signal exactly correct, and must make the correct visual signals at those times. It is allowed to fail to make the sound signal, but the visual signals must be on time. That is why it is important that you check the preparatory signal by watching the committee boat signals (or better still, listening to the time-keeper counting down to the preparatory signal, if you can get close enough); then you can rely on the starting signal being exactly four minutes later. (Rule 26)

When the race committee makes an 'individual recall' signal (when there are premature starters), it must not only display the visual signal (flag X) but also make a sound signal (an additional bang or horn). If it doesn't, and you are in doubt as to whether or not you are a premature starter, you may assume you have started correctly and sail on. If the race committee scores you as 'OCS' (On the Course Side at the start) you will be entitled to redress. If you are in no doubt that you are a premature starter, you must return to start properly, whether or not the race committee makes the correct signal. (Rule 29.1, ISAF Case 31)

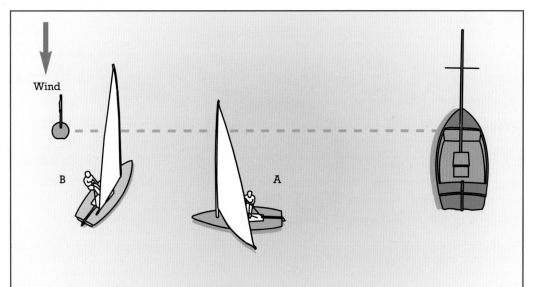

Wind

B

A

At the moment of the starting signal

You are A: You may want to luff to close-hauled but you may not. B is keeping clear and to luff now would deprive him of room to keep clear. (Rule 16.1)

You are B: You are the give-way boat, but your course and speed will mean you will pass safely ahead of A who is not allowed to change course if that deprives you of room to keep clear. Mind you, if there is an incident and he didn't luff, you'll be likely to lose the protest!

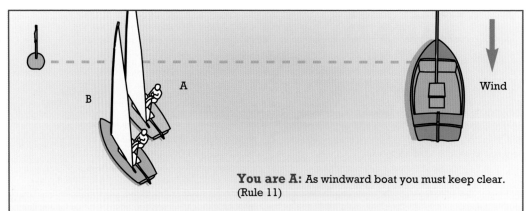

You are A: As windward boat you must keep clear. (Rule 11)

You are B: However you came to be overlapped, (you might have come from astern, or you might have tacked to leeward of A) you may luff (above close-hauled if necessary) to get round the mark, but you must give A room to keep clear. If you established the overlap from clear astern, then you mustn't sail above your proper course, so once you have passed the mark you must bear away to close-hauled or below.

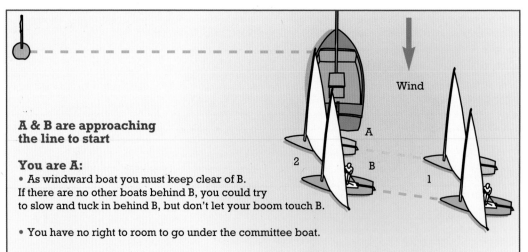

A & B are approaching the line to start

You are A:
• As windward boat you must keep clear of B.
If there are no other boats behind B, you could try to slow and tuck in behind B, but don't let your boom touch B.

• You have no right to room to go under the committee boat.

• Next time you want to start at the starboard end, don't get caught in this position!

You are B:
• Position 1: Before the starting signal, however the overlap was established, you may luff as high as you like, but if you change course you must give A room to keep clear. If you luff slowly now, A has got room to keep clear by sailing the wrong side of the committee boat. (Rules 11, 16 & 18.1(a))

• After the starting signal, if you established the overlap from clear astern, you must not luff higher than your 'proper course' (close-hauled or the course which takes you just astern of the committee boat). (Rule 17.1)

• If you sail a straight course which allows A enough room to sail astern of the committee boat, then to luff when he cannot escape would not be giving him room. So if you want to shut him out, you need to luff at position 1. (Rules 11, 16 & 18.1(a))

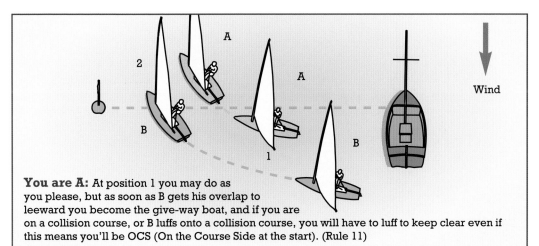

You are A: At position 1 you may do as
you please, but as soon as B gets his overlap to
leeward you become the give-way boat, and if you are
on a collision course, or B luffs onto a collision course, you will have to luff to keep clear even if
this means you'll be OCS (On the Course Side at the start). (Rule 11)

You are B:
• At position 1 you are the give-way boat and must keep clear. (Rule 12)

• When you first get the overlap you become the right-of-way boat, but you must not be so close
to A that he can't keep clear. (Rule 15)

• Before the starting signal you may luff up to head-to-wind but you must give A room to keep
clear (Rule 16)

• At the moment of the starting signal you must promptly bear away to a course no higher than
close-hauled. (Rule 17.1)

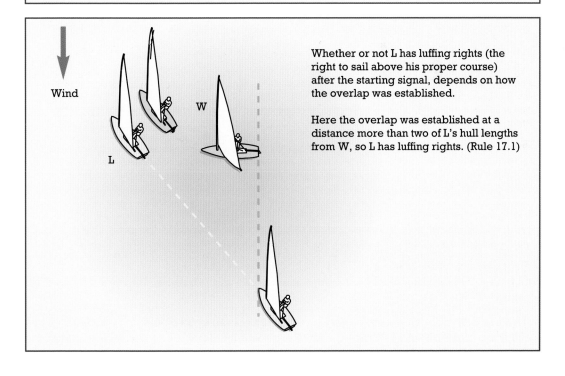

Whether or not L has luffing rights (the
right to sail above his proper course)
after the starting signal, depends on how
the overlap was established.

Here the overlap was established at a
distance more than two of L's hull lengths
from W, so L has luffing rights. (Rule 17.1)

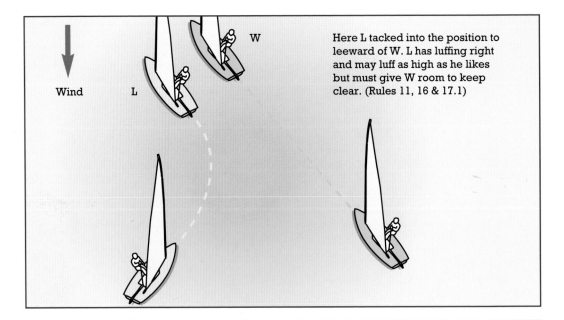

Wind   L   W   Here L tacked into the position to
                                                        leeward of W. L has luffing right
                                                        and may luff as high as he likes
                                                        but must give W room to keep
                                                        clear. (Rules 11, 16 & 17.1)

The diagram opposite shows a reaching start. Before the starting signal (when there is no proper course), all the leeward boats (B, D, F and H) may luff up to head-to-wind, if they can give room to the windward boats to keep clear. At the moment of the starting signal, a boat without luffing rights sailing higher than her proper course must bear away. Assuming that their proper courses are to the right of the picture, which of the leeward boats may luff (sail above their proper course) after the starting signal?

You are A or C or E or G: You must keep clear of the leeward boats under you; and you must keep clear of X coming down the start line on starboard tack, and you must not sail below your proper course after the starting signal. (Rules 11, 10, and 17.2)

You are B: You established your overlap from clear astern, but you were more than two lengths away from A at the time. You have luffing rights. You may sail higher than your proper course before or after the start - right up to head-to-wind if A can keep clear. But you must not luff A into the path of X, coming down the start line on starboard tack; in fact you might have to bear away and give more room to A. (Rules 11, 17.1 and 18.2(a))

You are D: You established your overlap from clear astern, and you were within two lengths of C at the time. You are the only leeward boat not to have luffing rights. Before the starting signal (when there is no proper course) you may sail as high as you like, but at the starting signal you must bear away if necessary and then mustn't sail higher than your proper course during the existence of the overlap (unless the gap between the two boats gets to be more than two lengths). (Rules 11 & 17.1)

You are F: E established the overlap to windward of you, so you have luffing rights. You may sail higher than your proper course after the start - right up to head-to-wind if E can keep clear. (Rule 11)

You are H: You established your overlap by completing a tack to leeward of G. You have luffing rights. You may sail higher than your proper course after the start - right up to head-to-wind if G can keep clear. (Rule 11)

You are X: You are not going to be very popular, but as you are on starboard tack you have right-of-way over all the other boats. 'Proper Course' is not relevant when boats are on opposite tacks. (Rule 10)

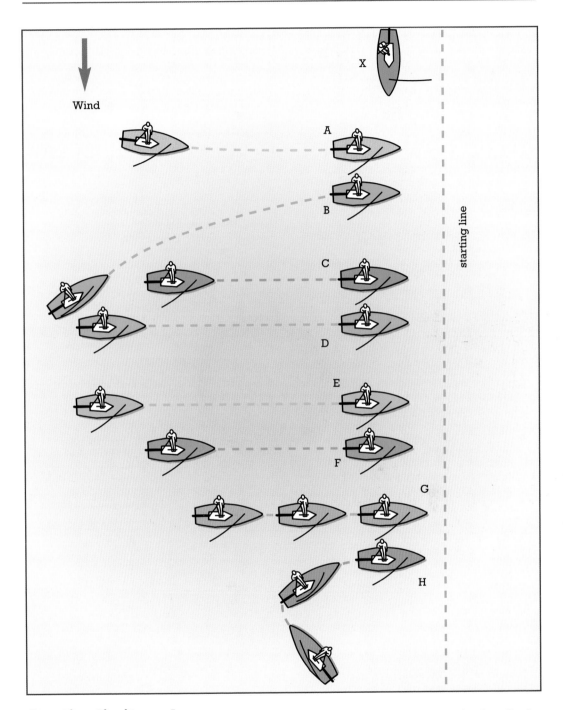

Starting limit marks

Most on-the-water starting lines are between a small buoy (the outer distance mark, or 'ODM') at the port end, and the mast of a committee boat at the starboard end. These must be described in the sailing instructions. Both the ODM and the committee boat are 'marks' because they have a 'required side' when boats start. The committee boat is also an obstruction, and an inside boat therefore has the right to room when everyone is milling about before the start, but not when boats are approaching the line to start. Then no one has the right to room at any starting mark (that is 'surrounded by navigable water').

The most common starting limit mark is the 'inner limit mark' or 'inner distance mark' ('IDM'). Not just the description of the IDM but also the obligations of boats with respect to it must be written into the sailing instructions. You can ignore a sailing instruction like 'There will be an IDM, which will be a yellow mark with a pink flag laid near to the committee boat'.

IDMs cause a lot of problems. The usual reasons one is used are to help protect the committee boat, and to keep boats from sailing very close to the committee boat, blocking the race committee's view of the starting line.

Let's look at three examples of a limit mark sailing instruction:

1 'A yellow mark with a pink flag will be laid near the committee boat. Boats shall not pass between this mark and the committee boat after the preparatory signal.'
Strictly speaking, such a sailing instruction does not give the mark a required side (rather it specifies a prohibited area which by definition is an obstruction) so it could be argued that you have the right to room to avoid the 'obstruction', and you may hit the buoy without penalty (provided you don't cross the imaginary line between it and any

part of the committee boat); and if you are forced into the 'prohibited area' by a boat breaking a rule you can escape penalty by protesting the boat that forced you to break the sailing instruction. (Rule 60.1(a) gives you the right to a hearing and Rule 64.1(b) exonerates you.)

2 The most sensible sailing instruction would be: 'A yellow mark with a pink flag will be laid near the committee boat. Boats approaching the line to start shall pass between this mark and the ODM' or 'boats shall pass this mark to starboard'. This would require you to pass the IDM on your starboard side when you are 'approaching the line to start from the pre-course side of the starting line'. Under this sailing instruction, the IDM is a mark because it has a required side, so there is no question of any right to room when you're approaching the line to start. If you get forced the wrong side by someone to leeward who has not broken a rule (for example by luffing you gently the wrong side of the mark), then you'll just have to sail back and unwind, and pass it on the correct side.

3 In an attempt to really discourage boats from the area between the IDM and the committee boat, the race committee might write a sailing instruction like this: 'A yellow mark with a pink flag will be placed near the committee boat. When approaching the line to start, boats shall pass between this mark and the ODM and after the preparatory signal boats shall not pass between this mark and the committee boat'. With this sailing instruction

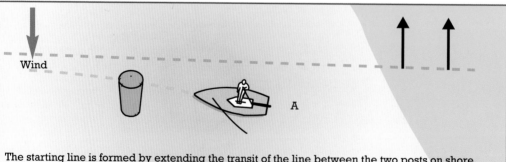

Wind

A

The starting line is formed by extending the transit of the line between the two posts on shore. The ODM has been placed to limit the length of the line.

You are A: When the ODM has drifted behind the line and the port end is favoured, you can gain an advantage. Having passed the ODM on your port side, you'll need to keep sailing towards the line ('approaching the line to start') until you start.

the IDM has a required side, so it is a mark. This means there's no right to room when approaching the line to start and if you get forced between the mark and the committee boat by a boat that didn't break a rule, then you'll have to retire. (I don't recommend such a draconian sailing instruction, but I often see them.)

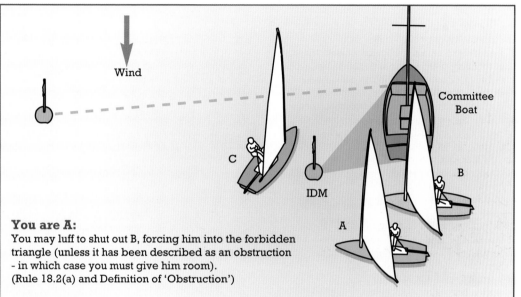

You are A:
You may luff to shut out B, forcing him into the forbidden triangle (unless it has been described as an obstruction - in which case you must give him room).
(Rule 18.2(a) and Definition of 'Obstruction')

You are B:
• You must keep clear of A and you cannot claim room if the IDM has a required side in the sailing instructions. However, if the area between the mark and the committee boat is simply a prohibited area, then A must give you room (whether you ask for it or not, but it's best to hail). (Rules 18.1(a) & 18.2(a) and Definition of 'Obstruction')

• If you hit the mark but pass it on the correct (starboard) side, you can exonerate yourself by sailing clear and doing a 360 if your only infringement was hitting the mark, or a 720 if you broke a 'when boats meet' rule (for example by not keeping clear of A). If you broke a 'when boats meet' rule *and* you hit the mark, a 720 will exonerate you for both.

• If you are forced the wrong side of the mark, then whether or not you can successfully protest A, or exonerate yourself, all depends on the wording of the sailing instruction.

You are C:
If this is the best end to start and the IDM is behind the line you can gain something here by starting right at the end of the line. But having passed the IDM on your starboard side, you must keep sailing towards the line (or you're no longer 'approaching the line to start') and if the sailing instruction prohibits you from sailing between the IDM and the committee boat, you'll need to keep out of the prohibited triangle.

5 The Gate Start

Gate starts are becoming more common in some parts of the world as a way of starting more than eighty or so boats, in a fairly steady wind of Force 3 or more, when there is sufficient room on the water. Discussion will never cease as to whether the gate start or the line start is the fairer, but there is no doubt that to get a good gate start skippers need different skills and experience. Gate starts can be exciting, and fun.

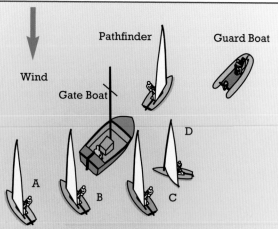

This is how a gate start works. A pathfinder is appointed. Usually it is one of the competing boats near the top of the fleet. Just before the starting signal he sets off on a port tack close-hauled course. A guard boat is sometimes used, to motor along on the pathfinder's starboard bow, to ensure other boats don't run into the pathfinder and ruin the proceedings.

A gate boat takes up a position astern of the pathfinder, exactly matching the pathfinder's speed and course. Boats then start on starboard tack behind the gate boat. Those that think they sail faster than the pathfinder, or think the left side of the beat is best, start early (near the beginning of the run). Those that think the pathfinder sails faster than they do, or think the right side of the beat is best, wait around where they expect the entourage to be, five minutes or so after the starting signal. Knowing the exact time is unimportant; the skill is in 'coming out of the gate' close-hauled at full speed by luffing from a reach to close-hauled, missing the starboard quarter of the gate-boat by a few millimetres. The pathfinder is usually released after five minutes; he can tack any time after being released, gaining a few boat lengths by not having to sail behind the gate boat - a reward for being forced to start at the extreme right side of the beat, and not being allowed to tack on any shifts for the first five minutes of the race.

You are A or B:
• This is really just the same situation as the starboard end of a fixed starting line. You have to keep clear of a boat to leeward, and you have right-of-way over a boat to windward. You must also keep clear of the gate boat.

You are C:
• If you can sail close-hauled without changing course, then you can ignore D. Or you can luff D to force him to luff alongside the gate boat, but you can't luff him into the gate boat, because if you luff you must give him room to keep clear. (Rule 16)

You are D:
• You will need to slow, not to go behind C as you would if this were a fixed-line start, but to be level with him, as are A and B. Remember, the gate-boat is moving at the speed of the pathfinder. You must keep clear of the gate boat. If you touch the gate boat (or the guard boat or - heaven forbid - the pathfinder), you must retire (no chance of a 720) unless you think it wasn't your fault. For example if C forces you to collide with the gate boat by luffing you can hail 'protest', sail on, and lodge a protest after the race.

6 On the Beat

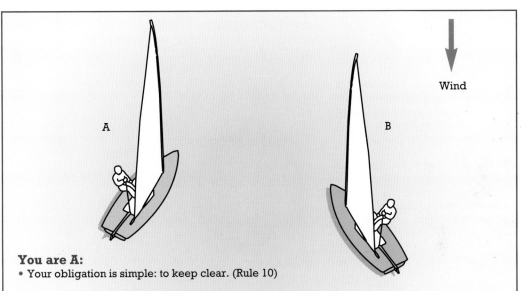

You are A:
* Your obligation is simple: to keep clear. (Rule 10)

* If you are going to bear away behind B, you must do it in such a way that B is not left in doubt that you are going to succeed. (Rule 10)

If you decide to tack, you must complete the tack ahead or to leeward of B without B having to change course to keep clear until your tack is complete. If there is doubt about whether you tacked far enough from B, a protest hearing is likely to go against you. (Rules 13 & 15)

You are B:
* If you change course you must give room to A to keep clear. Furthermore, if A is keeping clear by ducking your stern you mustn't change course if as a result A would immediately need to change course to continue keeping clear. (Rule 16)

* You are not required to hail 'starboard' or anything else, but it is sometimes a good idea to do so if you think that A hasn't seen you because:

1. You must try to avoid contact, and if there is contact and there is damage, you may be penalised. (Rule 14)

2. Even if there is no chance of damage, getting tangled up with a boat required to keep clear can cost many boat-lengths and no redress can be claimed for places lost (unless you are actually damaged by the give-way boat). (Rules 14, 16 & 62.1(b))

* If you want to continue on starboard tack, and don't want A tacking into a position which forces you (from a tactical point of view) to tack, you may bear away and go behind A. You could shout 'Carry on', or 'Pass ahead of me' but nothing you shout puts any obligation on A which he doesn't already have. Although an early bear-away and/or a hail will often make A decide to carry on, if A is an experienced and skilled racing sailor and is determined to force you into a tactically disadvantageous position, it is not easy to prevent him.

When A completes his tack he is overlapped to leeward of B

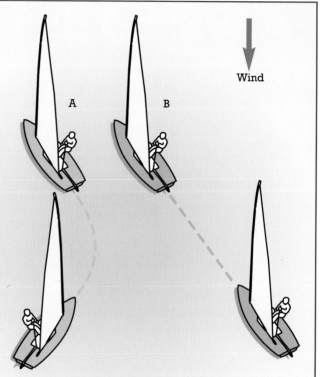

Wind

You are A:
• As you approach on port tack, and while luffing to head-to-wind, your obligation is simple - to keep clear of B. (Rule 10)

• When you pass through head-to-wind and until you are close-hauled on the new tack you must continue to keep clear of B. (Rule 13)

• When your tack is complete, you become the right-of-way boat, but it is only at that instant that B has to begin to take any avoiding action, so you mustn't be in a position where it is impossible or difficult for B to keep clear. Remember that he doesn't have to anticipate that you are going to be there. If he is able to keep clear only by making an unseamanlike manoeuvre, then your tack was too close. (Rule 15)

• When your tack is complete, you become the right-of-way boat and you have luffing rights, but you cannot use them until you have given B room to keep clear (which requires both space and time). After giving B this opportunity, you may luff above close-hauled if you want to, but your luff must be such that B is able to keep clear. (Rule 16)

You are B:
• You must not change course if by so doing you prevent A from keeping clear, or force him to make an unseamanlike manoeuvre in order to keep clear. If there is a header (adverse windshift) just as A is tacking, you may be prevented from fulfilling your wish to bear away for a few seconds. You may, of course, tack while A is tacking. (Rule 16)

• You may change course towards A as he approaches on port tack (whether or not there is a windshift), forcing A to tack earlier, provided you give him room to keep clear. (Rule 16)

• You don't have to anticipate A becoming the right-of-way boat. Other than to avoid contact, you are not required to alter course to avoid him until his tack is complete.

• Once A's tack is complete and he is to leeward, you become the give-way boat, and you must keep clear even if he luffs. If he executed a good 'lee bow', and you will be affected by his back-wind, it's usually tactically sound to tack. (Rule 11)

• Remember that A has luffing rights; once he has given you the opportunity to keep clear he may luff.

• You are not prohibited from tacking, even if A has changed course to keep clear, provided that you give A room to keep clear.

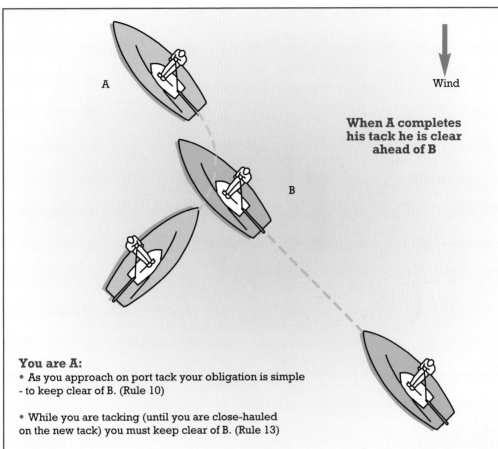

When A completes his tack he is clear ahead of B

You are A:
• As you approach on port tack your obligation is simple
- to keep clear of B. (Rule 10)

• While you are tacking (until you are close-hauled
on the new tack) you must keep clear of B. (Rule 13)

• When your tack is complete you become the right-of-way boat, but it is only at that instant that B has to begin to take any avoiding action, so you mustn't be in a position where B doesn't have room to keep clear. Remember that he doesn't have to anticipate that you are going to be there. If he is able to keep clear only by making an unseamanlike manoeuvre, then your tack was too close. (Rule 15)

• When you complete your tack you may be sailing more slowly than B, and if B establishes an overlap to leeward of you, you become the give-way boat again, and you must keep clear. (Rule 11)

You are B:
• You must not change course if by so doing you prevent A from keeping clear, or force him to make an unseamanlike manoeuvre in order to keep clear. If there is a lift (beneficial windshift) just as A is passing ahead, you may be prevented from fulfilling your wish to luff for a few seconds. (Rule 16)

• Provided you don't deprive A of room to keep clear, you can tack away at any time. If you get an overlap to leeward of A, after his tack is complete, you may not sail above close hauled unless you promptly sail astern of A (for example to tack away). (Rule 17.1)

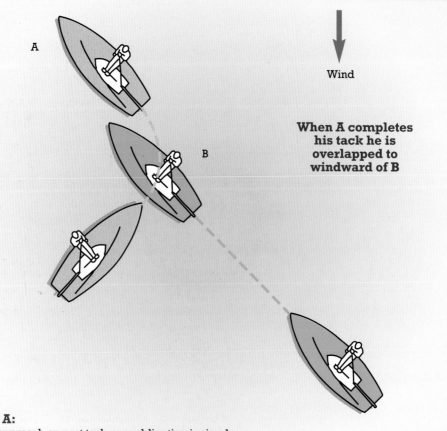

When A completes his tack he is overlapped to windward of B

You are A:
• As you approach on port tack your obligation is simple
- to keep clear of B. (Rule 10)

• While you are tacking (until you are close-hauled on the new tack)
you must keep clear of B. (Rule 13)

• When your tack is complete, you are overlapped on B's windward bow putting B in your wind shadow. The manoeuvre is known as a 'slam dunk'. You are still the give-way boat. Furthermore, B has luffing rights and may luff above close-hauled, and you must keep clear. (Rule 11)

• At the completion of your tack you must not be so close to B that B cannot luff without immediately making contact with you. (Rule 11, Definition of 'Keep Clear')

You are B:
• You are the right-of-way boat throughout this manoeuvre, and unless you change course, you do not need to give A room to keep clear. If there is a lift (beneficial windshift) just as A is passing ahead, you may be prevented from fulfilling your wish to luff for a few seconds. (Rule 16)

• At the completion of A's tack you are overlapped to leeward of A, so you have luffing rights, and may luff above close-hauled, but if you luff you must give A room to keep clear. (Rule 16)

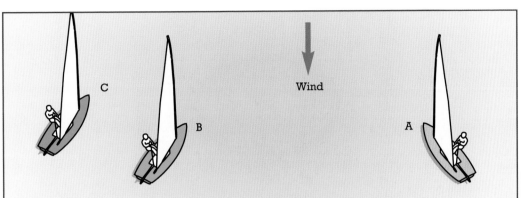

You are A:
• Your rights and obligations are exactly the same as those of boat B on page 29.

You are B:
• You must keep clear of A. (Rule 10)

• You have the right to choose either to go under A's stern or, as you need to change course substantially to avoid A, to tack, irrespective of any hail from C. (Rule 19.1 & Definition of 'Obstruction')

• If you decide to go behind A, you must allow C room to pass under A's stern should he also choose to do so (though unless you are in a team race and C is an opponent, he'd probably rather tack). (Rule 18.2(a))

• If you decide to tack, you must hail C for room to tack (something like 'room to tack' or 'water for a starboard boat') and then tack as soon as you can do so without colliding with C. You need to hail early enough to allow C time to respond to your hail before you have a problem with A. This is especially important if there are boats to windward of C. (Rule 19.1)

• You must not hail C for room to tack, and then go behind A (unless C does not respond to the hail). (Rule 19.1)

• If you decide to hail for room to tack, and C does not respond, hail again more loudly. The pivotal issues in a protest in relation to this situation are often whether or not the hail was made and if it was, whether it was in time for C to respond; typically the helmsman of the leeward boat says he hailed, and the helmsman of the hailed boat says he didn't hear a hail. The protest committee will be more inclined to find as fact that a hail was made if it has been repeated more loudly.

• If you can keep clear of A by making only a small (or no) change of course, then you do not have the right to hail and must pass under A, giving room to C if he chooses to go under A as well. (Rules 18.2(a), 19.1, Definition of Obstruction, ISAF Case 3)

You are C:
• Obviously you may tack if you want to.

• You must keep clear of A, and as windward boat you must keep clear of B if he luffs. If B sails behind A, then provided that in your opinion (you must be reasonable) you cannot safely cross in front of A, you have the right to go behind A, and B must give you room (whether or not you ask for it) provided you had an inside overlap when B was two lengths from A. (Rules 10, 11 & 18)

• If B hails for room to tack, then you must either immediately tack, or hail 'you tack' and take on the responsibility of keeping clear. If you choose to tack, you don't have to carry out the tack any faster than is normal for you, but you must begin the manoeuvre immediately. If there are boats to windward of you preventing you from tacking, you must hail them for room and tack when it is safe to do so. You are under no obligation to tack unless and until B hails for room. (Rule 19.1)

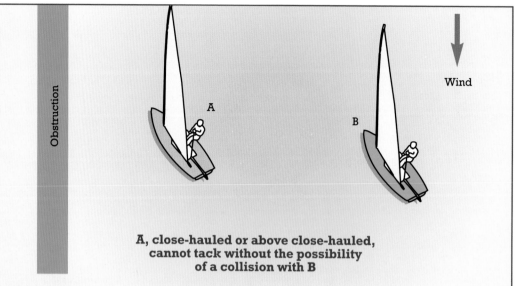

Obstruction

Wind

A

B

**A, close-hauled or above close-hauled,
cannot tack without the possibility
of a collision with B**

You are A:

• You will need room to tack, and you know that if you do B will be in the way, so you have the right to hail B for room to tack. (Rule 19.1)

• You are permitted to hail only if you really believe there is an obstruction ahead, but underwater weed or shallows count as an obstruction. (Definition of 'obstruction')

• Until you hail, B is under no obligation to do anything. (Rule 19.1)

• If he doesn't respond to the first hail, hail again more loudly.

• If there is a boat to windward or astern of B that would prevent him from tacking, you will need to hail in time for him to hail for room. (Rule 19.1)

• If he responds by tacking, you must tack as soon as possible even if there is a lift (advantageous windshift) and you'd like to change your mind and continue sailing near the shore out of an adverse tide. (Rule 19.1(a))

• If he responds by hailing 'you tack', you must tack as soon as possible. (Rule 19.1(b))

You are B:

• You must keep clear if A luffs to head-to-wind because you will be windward or astern. (Rules 11 & 12)

• Although you are under no obligation to do anything until A hails, if it's windy and noisy, you should be reasonably attentive to his need to hail.

• In response to his hail you must either tack as soon as possible or immediately hail back 'you tack'.

• If you want to tack but cannot tack because of a boat to windward or astern, you must hail that boat for room to tack and tack as soon as possible. (Rule 19)

• If you hail 'you tack' you must keep clear of A while he tacks, and having completed his tack, you have to give him room to keep clear. (Rule 19.1(b))

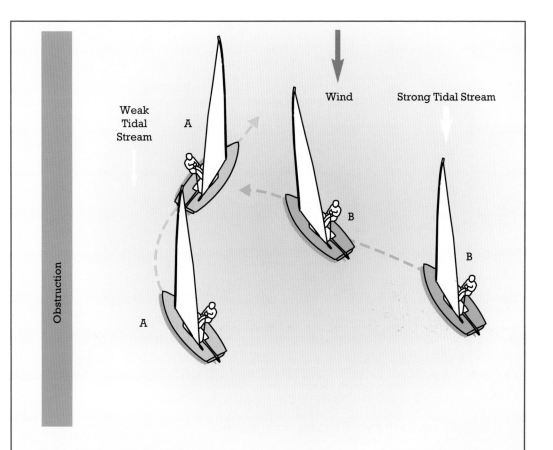

**A wants to tack but is unsure whether he can tack and clear B.
So A has the right to hail B for room to tack. A hails 'Room to tack'.
B replies 'You tack'**

You are A:
• Having hailed for room to tack, you must tack immediately there is room, even if there is a lift (advantageous windshift) and you'd like to continue sailing near the shore out of the adverse tidal stream. (Rule 19.1(a))

• When you have completed your tack you become the give-way boat and you must try to keep clear of B. In this diagram there is nothing you can do except sail straight on, so you can sail on and you have broken no rule. (Rules 10 and 19.1(b))

You are B:
When you hail 'You tack' you undertake to keep clear of A while he tacks, and having completed his tack, you must give him room to keep clear. You can give A room by bearing off behind him. If you do so, no rule is broken. (Rule 19.1(b))

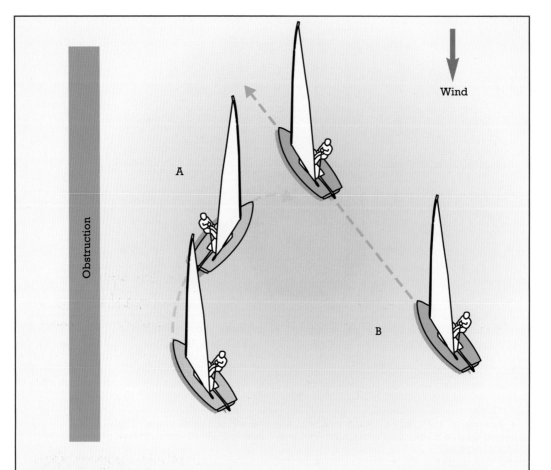

A wants to tack but is unsure whether he can tack and clear B. So A has the right to hail B for room to tack. A hails 'Room to tack'. B replies 'You tack'

You are A:
• Having hailed for room to tack, you must tack immediately there is room, even if there is a lift (advantageous windshift) and you'd like to continue sailing near the shore out of the adverse tidal stream. (Rule 19.1(a))

• When you have completed your tack you become the give-way boat and you must try to keep clear of B. If you can bear away under B's stern without difficulty (as you can in this diagram), then you must do so. You become required to keep clear only when your tack is complete, and if you then cannot keep clear, or you manage to keep clear only by making an unseamanlike manoeuvre, then B has broken Rule 19 and you should protest. (Rules 10 & 19.1(b)))

You are B:
When you hail 'You tack' you undertake to keep clear of A while he tacks, but having completed his tack, you have to give him room to keep clear. In this diagram you have done so; A can easily bear off behind you, so no rule is broken. (Rules 10 & 19.1(b))

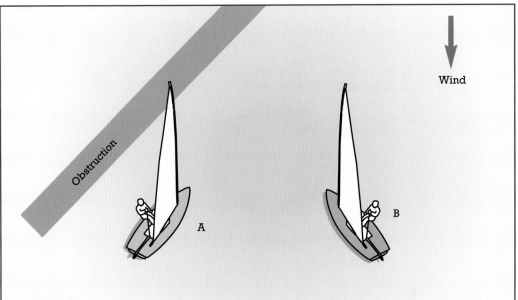

You are A:
• You are in big trouble. You don't have the right to room, and the obstruction prevents you from tacking. If you force B to change course, you must take a 'Two-Turns Penalty'. (Rules 10 & 44.1)

• You should have thought of this possibility earlier when there was time to bear away under B!

You are B:
• You could be Mr. Nice Guy and tack now, or you could sail on till you are forced to tack to avoid contact with A, in which case A will have broken Rule 10 and must take a penalty. (Rules 10 & 44.1)

7 Rounding the Windward Mark

Rounding a port-hand windward mark

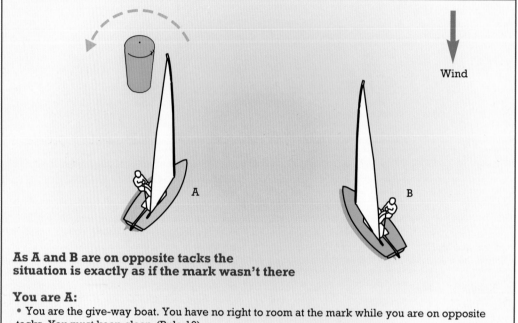

Wind

As A and B are on opposite tacks the situation is exactly as if the mark wasn't there

You are A:
• You are the give-way boat. You have no right to room at the mark while you are on opposite tacks. You must keep clear. (Rule 10)

• As you will see from the next few scenarios, it is risky to approach the mark so high on the layline if you are going to be on a collision course with a starboard-tack boat.

You are B:
• You are the right-of-way boat, but if you change course you must give room to A to keep clear. (Rule 16)

A tacks into a position overlapped to leeward of B, completing his tack when more than two lengths from the mark

You are A:
• As you approach on port tack, you are the give-way boat and must keep clear. (Rule 10)

• While you are tacking you are the give-way boat and must keep clear. (Rule 13)

• You have completed the tack just outside the two-length zone and you are overlapped inside B. You have tacked into this right-of-way position and B is not required to anticipate your becoming the

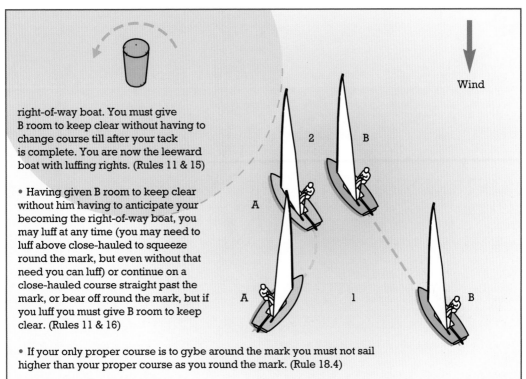

right-of-way boat. You must give B room to keep clear without having to change course till after your tack is complete. You are now the leeward boat with luffing rights. (Rules 11 & 15)

• Having given B room to keep clear without him having to anticipate your becoming the right-of-way boat, you may luff at any time (you may need to luff above close-hauled to squeeze round the mark, but even without that need you can luff) or continue on a close-hauled course straight past the mark, or bear off round the mark, but if you luff you must give B room to keep clear. (Rules 11 & 16)

• If your only proper course is to gybe around the mark you must not sail higher than your proper course as you round the mark. (Rule 18.4)

• If B is not able to keep clear while you luff to pass the mark because there are several other boats to windward of him, then you do not have the right to tack under him and sail your proper course round the mark. (Rule 18.2(d))

• If there is 'reasonable doubt' as to whether either of you were two lengths from the mark when your tack was complete, you must presume that you are too late to get the right to round inside B. (Rule 18.2(e))

• If having given room to B to keep clear at the completion of your tack, you need to luff to squeeze around the mark, you can luff to head-to-wind as quickly as you like. (Rule 18.2(d)

You are B:
• While A is approaching on port tack and while he's tacking you mustn't change course to prevent him from keeping clear. This doesn't stop you bearing away early to force him to tack earlier to avoid you, provided he can do it without difficulty. (Rules 13 & 16)

• If you are forced to change course to avoid A before he has completed his tack, he will have broken Rule 13.

• However, provided that A completes his tack outside the two-length zone, he becomes the right of way boat, and you must keep clear. He has luffing rights and unless his only proper course is to gybe around the mark, he may luff at any time as high as he likes, or sail straight on. You must keep clear. (Rules 11 & 18.2(a))

• If A's tack was completed when either of you were within two lengths of the mark, then A has no right to force you to sail above close-hauled. You can protest but you must still keep clear if you can. (Rules 18.2(e), 18.3(a) & 11)

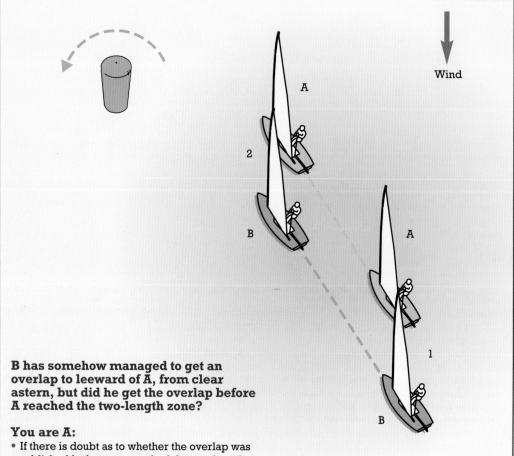

B has somehow managed to get an overlap to leeward of A, from clear astern, but did he get the overlap before A reached the two-length zone?

You are A:
• If there is doubt as to whether the overlap was established before you reached the two-length zone, then B does not have the right to round inside. It is a good idea to tell him so, and keep clear. (Rule 18.2(e))

• Because B got his overlap from clear astern, he has no luffing rights, but if the overlap is established before you reached the two-length zone, then he may sail his proper course around the mark, and you must keep clear. His proper course is a wide rounding if that's how he would round without your being there. You must keep clear. (Rule 18.2(a))

You are B:
• If the boats become overlapped, without doubt, before A reaches the two-lengths zone, and are overlapped at the two-length zone, you have the right to sail your proper course as you round the mark. This means you may sail the course you would have sailed in the absence of A, even if this means sailing above close-hauled to 'shoot' the mark. You may even head up a bit so that you don't get too far from the mark as you complete the rounding. (Rule 18.2(a))

• If there is 'reasonable doubt' as to whether A was two hull-lengths from the mark when you established the overlap, you must presume that you are too late. If A is shouting to you that your overlap is too late, you'd be wise to keep clear. (Rule 18.2(e))

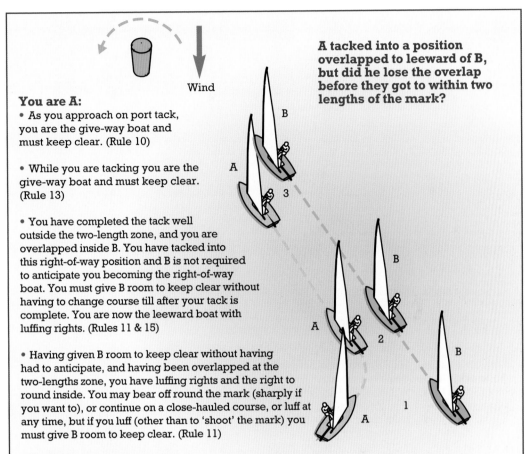

Wind

A tacked into a position overlapped to leeward of B, but did he lose the overlap before they got to within two lengths of the mark?

You are A:
• As you approach on port tack, you are the give-way boat and must keep clear. (Rule 10)

• While you are tacking you are the give-way boat and must keep clear. (Rule 13)

• You have completed the tack well outside the two-length zone, and you are overlapped inside B. You have tacked into this right-of-way position and B is not required to anticipate you becoming the right-of-way boat. You must give B room to keep clear without having to change course till after your tack is complete. You are now the leeward boat with luffing rights. (Rules 11 & 15)

• Having given B room to keep clear without having had to anticipate, and having been overlapped at the two-lengths zone, you have luffing rights and the right to round inside. You may bear off round the mark (sharply if you want to), or continue on a close-hauled course, or luff at any time, but if you luff (other than to 'shoot' the mark) you must give B room to keep clear. (Rule 11)

• Only if your only proper course is to gybe around the mark must you not sail higher than your proper course as you round the mark. (Rule 18.4)

• If there is 'reasonable doubt' as to whether either of you had reached the two-length zone when your tack was complete, you must not force B to sail above close-hauled. (Rules 18.2(e), 18.3(a))

You are B:
• While A is approaching on port tack and while he's tacking you mustn't change course to prevent him from keeping clear or make it difficult for him to keep clear, or force him to immediately alter course. This doesn't stop you bearing away early to force him to tack earlier to avoid you, provided he can keep clear without difficulty. (Rules 13 & 16)

• If you are forced to change course before A has completed his tack, A will have broken Rule 13.

• As A completes his tack outside the two-length zone, he becomes the right of way boat, and you must keep clear. He has luffing rights and unless his only proper course is to gybe around the mark, he may luff at any time or sail straight on. You must keep clear. (Rules 11 & 18.2(a))

• If there is doubt as to whether you have broken the overlap when you reached the two-length zone, then A has the right to room. If A is shouting to you that he is overlapped at two lengths, you'd be wise to keep clear. (Rule 18.2(e))

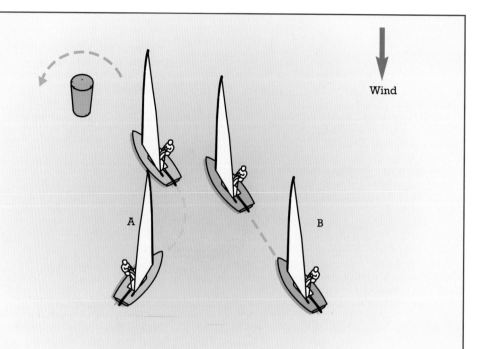

A completes his tack onto starboard within two lengths of the mark, ahead or to leeward of B

You are A:

• As you approach on port tack, you are the give-way boat and must keep clear. (Rule 10)

• While you are tacking you are the give-way boat and must keep clear. (Rule 13)

• You have completed the tack within the two-length zone. You have tacked into this right-of-way position but B is not required to anticipate your having become the right-of-way boat. You must give B room to keep clear without having to change course till after your tack is complete. (Rule 15)

• Now you have another problem. Even after your tack is complete, you must not force B (who is probably sailing faster than you are) to luff above close-hauled in order to avoid you. (Rule 18.3(a))

You are B:

• While A is approaching on port tack and while he's tacking you mustn't change course to prevent him from keeping clear or make it difficult for him to keep clear. This doesn't stop you bearing away early to force him to tack earlier to avoid you, provided he can keep clear without difficulty. (Rules 13 & 16)

• If you are forced to change course before A has completed his tack, A will have broken Rule 13.

• If A completes his tack to leeward of you he becomes the right of way boat, but if you can avoid him only by sailing above close-hauled (which is almost inevitable in this diagram) then he has broken Rule 18.3(a) and must take a penalty.

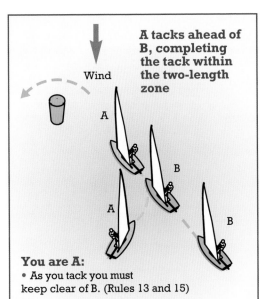

A tacks ahead of B, completing the tack within the two-length zone

Wind

You are A:
• As you tack you must keep clear of B. (Rules 13 and 15)

• If you complete your tack without forcing B to change course to avoid you, the next thing you have to worry about is that if B, with superior speed, can avoid you only by sailing above his close-hauled course, then you have broken a rule, and must take a penalty. (Rules 15 & 18.3(a))

• Furthermore, if B chooses to bear away and gets an overlap to leeward of you, you must keep clear while B rounds the mark. (Rule 18.3(b))

• Whatever you do you mustn't prevent B from passing the mark. (Rule 18.3(a))

• Basically, for this manoeuvre to succeed, you must stay clear ahead until B has rounded or passed the mark (that is, until B has left the mark astern).

You are B:
• When A's tack is complete, you become the give-way boat, but if the only way you can avoid him is to luff above your close-hauled course, he has broken a rule and must take a penalty. (Rule 18.3(a))

• If you choose to bear away and get an overlap to leeward of A, A must keep clear while you round or pass the mark. You mustn't sail higher than your proper course. Rules 17.1 & 18.3(b))

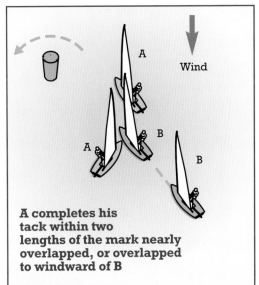

Wind

A completes his tack within two lengths of the mark nearly overlapped, or overlapped to windward of B

You are A:
• As you tack you must keep clear of B. (Rules 13 and 15)

• If at the moment you pass through head-to-wind B is overlapped to leeward, then B has luffing rights. You must continue to keep clear of B even if B luffs right up to head-to-wind. (Rule 11)

• If at the moment your tack is complete B is clear astern, and chooses to go between you and the mark, you must give room to B who is allowed to sail his proper course (the course he would have sailed had you not been there). (Rule 18.3(b))

You are B:
• If you were clear astern when A completed his tack, you may choose to go inside if you want to, and then sail your proper course (the course you would have sailed had A not been there) and if you need to luff above close hauled you do not need to give room to A to keep clear. (Rules 18.3(b) & 18.3(d))

• If you were overlapped to leeward of A when A completed his tack, you have luffing rights and you may sail any course, but if you luff above your proper course you must give A room to keep clear. However, if your only proper course is to gybe at the mark, you can sail your proper course but no higher. (Rules 11, 16, 18.4 & 18.3(d))

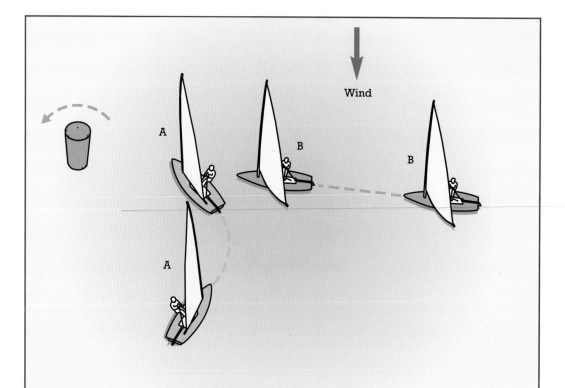

A tacks, completing his tack within two lengths of the mark to leeward or ahead of B who is approaching on a reach (perhaps having overstood the mark)

You are A:
• You must complete your tack without forcing B to change course to keep clear. (Rule 13)

• After you have completed your tack, you are the right-of-way boat but you mustn't be in a position that forces B to sail above his close-hauled course in order to keep clear of you. (Rule 18.3(a))

• Even though you have luffing rights, you must not prevent B from passing the mark. (Rule 18.3(a))

• Once B has passed the mark (left it astern) you may luff (you have luffing rights) but if you do you must give B room to keep clear. (Rules 11 & 16)

You are B:
• You need do nothing till A's tack is complete, then you must keep clear, but if the only way you can keep clear is by sailing above close-hauled, then A must take a Two-Turns Penalty. (Rule 18.3(a))

Rounding a starboard-hand windward mark

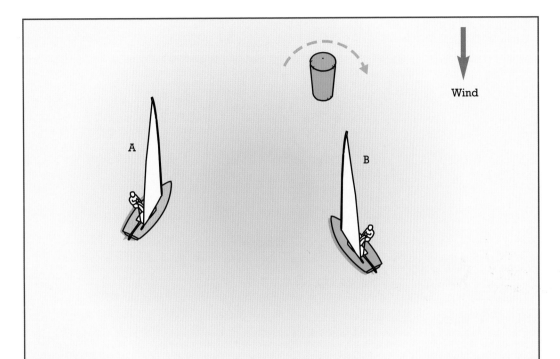

A and B are on opposite tacks so the situation is exactly as if the mark wasn't there

You are A:
You are the give-way boat. You have no right to room at the mark. You must keep clear. (Rule 10)

You are B:
You hold right-of-way, but if you change course you must give A room to keep clear. (Rule 16)

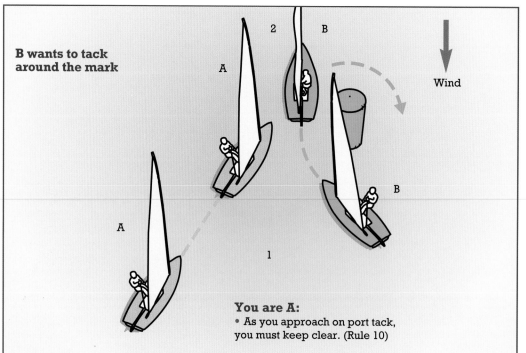

B wants to tack around the mark

Wind

You are A:
• As you approach on port tack, you must keep clear. (Rule 10)

• At position 2, B has luffed to head-to-wind. He is still on starboard tack. You must keep clear. (Rule 10)

• If you keep clear by luffing, you must not end up so close alongside him that any change of course he makes will result in immediately making contact. (Rule 10 and the Definition of 'Keep Clear'.)

• If you luff and tack, you must keep clear. (Rule 13)

You are B:
• As A approaches you must not change course so as to make it difficult for A to keep clear. However, the luff to get to position 2 has fulfilled this obligation, as A can easily keep clear by luffing. (Rule 16)

• At position 2 you must not turn any more, because once you go through head-to-wind you become the give-way boat, and A is so close behind that he will be forced to change course. (Rule 13)

• If A ducks your stern, leaving the mark on the wrong side, you'll probably be able to tack but you will be the give-way boat while you're tacking, and you'll probably be the windward boat when you've completed your tack. In either case you must keep clear. (Rules 13 & 11)

• If A luffs to avoid you when you're head-to-wind, and gets overlapped on your port side, although you remain the right-of-way boat till he goes through head-to-wind, if you bear away you must give him room to keep clear. (Rule 16)

• If A tacks, then immediately he is past head-to-wind you can complete your tack. (Rule 13)

• The best tactic in this scenario if you haven't room to complete a tack before A gets too close, is to slow down at position 1 to force A to tack, then tack.

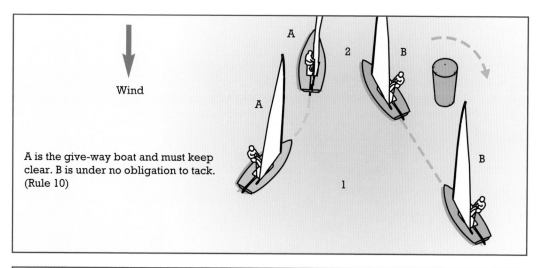

A is the give-way boat and must keep clear. B is under no obligation to tack. (Rule 10)

You are A:
You were keeping clear of B by passing ahead. B has altered course so he must give you room to keep clear. (Rule 16)

You are B:
As much as you may like to luff to tack around the mark, you cannot do this if the change of course doesn't give A room to keep clear. (Rule 16)

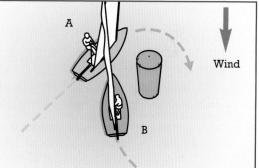

You are A:
• At position 1 when you begin to luff to tack, you are clear ahead and, therefore, the right-of-way boat.

• When you go through head-to-wind you must keep clear of B. Because B has luffed you may be prevented from completing your tack. (Rule 13)

• Next time you approach the mark with an opponent close astern, try to be on the layline, rather than half a length to leeward.

You are B:
• As A luffs to head-to-wind, you may luff too. You don't have to anticipate that he is going to tack.

• When A goes through head-to-wind you become the right-of-way boat, so if you change course after he goes through head-to-wind, you must give him room to keep clear. In the diagram he does have room - he can bear away. (Rules 12, 10 & 16)

• To prevent A from tacking in front of you, you need to luff till he reaches head-to-wind, then sail straight. Tack when there's room.

When the windward mark is an obstruction

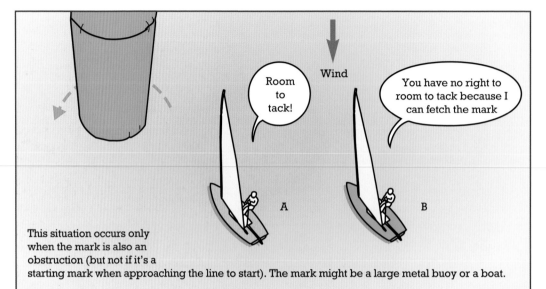

This situation occurs only
when the mark is also an
obstruction (but not if it's a
starting mark when approaching the line to start). The mark might be a large metal buoy or a boat.

You are A:
• Provided that you need to make more than a minor change of course to avoid the obstruction, you may hail to B for room to tack. 'Water' may be misunderstood; 'Room to tack' is best. (Rule 19.1)

• If B chooses not to tack, and then fails to fetch the mark (that is, he goes beyond head-to-wind to get round), then he has broken a rule and you should protest him. (Rule 19.2)

• Even if B can get round the mark without going beyond head-to-wind, you are still the right-of-way boat provided you don't go beyond head-to-wind yourself, so even if you don't have luffing rights, you may go up to head-to-wind in order to 'shoot the mark', and B must keep clear. (Rule 11 & Definition of 'Proper Course')

• For you to have the right to hail, you have to be on a course from which you must make a substantial change to avoid the obstruction. If you were further to leeward, so that the obstruction was not in your path, then you would not have the right to hail; you would have to slow down and tack behind B or bear off and gybe. (Definition of 'obstruction')

• If you do hail for room to tack, you must tack as soon as there is room. You can't hail and then 'shoot the mark' by going head-to-wind and bearing away around the mark. (Rule 19.1)

You are B:
• As the windward boat you must keep clear if A luffs in an attempt to 'shoot the mark'. If he luffs to shoot the mark he does not have to give you room to keep clear. (Rules 11 & 18.2(d))

• If A hails for room to tack, and you are sure that you can get round the mark without tacking, then you may refuse to tack, but if he luffs remember you are the windward boat and must keep clear. (Rule 11)

• If A hails for room to tack, and you are not sure that you can get round the mark without tacking, then you must either tack or hail back 'you tack' and give room to A to tack. (Rule 19)

8 On the Reach

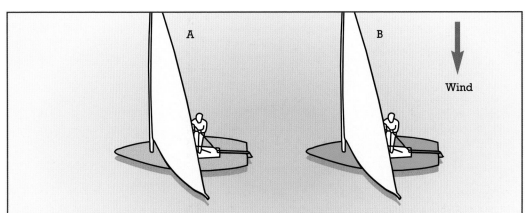

You are A: You are the right-of-way boat and you may change course as you please. (Rule 12)

You are B: Your only obligation is to keep clear of A (because you are 'clear astern'), but you may sail any course you like. (Rule 12)

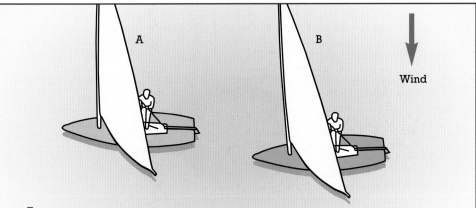

You are A:
• If B is within two hull-lengths of you and heading towards your leeward side, you must not sail below your proper course (see the definition of proper course on pages 12 & 13). (Rule 17.2)

• Remeber, if there are waves to be played, you can play them. If there are boats to windward or astern likely to take your wind, you can luff or bear away to get clear air. You simply mustn't sail lower than you would have done in the absence of B. (Rules 12 & 17.2)

You are B:
• As you are the boat clear astern, you must keep clear of A, but while there is no overlap you have no other obligations and may change course as you please. (Rule 12)

You are A:

• After B gets an overlap, you continue to be required not to sail below your proper course, but you now have a new obligation - to keep clear, even if B sails a course higher than your own. (Rules 17.2 & 11)

• If B sails a course you think is higher than his proper course, you may protest, but you must still keep clear. (Rule 11)

• If B sails very low (perhaps in an effort to hold on to clear wind), you continue to be obliged not to sail below your proper course while the gap between you is anything up to two hull-lengths. (Rules 11 & 17.2)

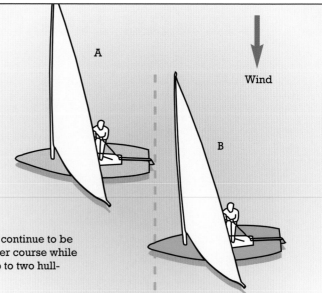

You are B:

• When you get your overlap to leeward of A, you will become the right-of-way boat, but A doesn't have to anticipate your getting the overlap, so you must initially give him room to keep clear. You mustn't get the overlap so close to his quarter, that if he luffed there would immediately be contact. (Rule 15 & Definition of 'Keep Clear')

• Once you've got an overlap, although you don't have luffing rights, you may sail up to, but not above, your proper course. You must not sail above your proper course while the overlap exists and you are within two hull-lengths of A. If there are other boats coming up behind, your proper course may be to luff. (Rules 11 & 17.1)

• If you luff (up to your proper course), you must give A room to keep clear. (Rule 16)

B having established an overlap to leeward of A, has somehow advanced nearly a boat-length through A's lee. There is no change in rights and obligations. B may sail as high as his proper course, and A must keep clear. A might be forced to sail higher than his own proper course, but nevertheless he must keep clear.

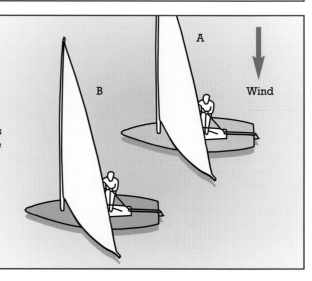

The boats are in the same positions as they were in the previous diagram, but here the situation has arisen through A establishing an overlap from astern to windward of B. The boats' rights and obligations are quite different, because B has luffing rights.

You are A:
• You must keep clear of B. (Rule 11)

• You must not sail below your proper course whilst the overlap exits (and the gap between the two boats is less than two hull-lengths). (Rule 17.2)

You are B:
• You may sail any course but if you luff you must give A room to keep clear. (Rule 16)

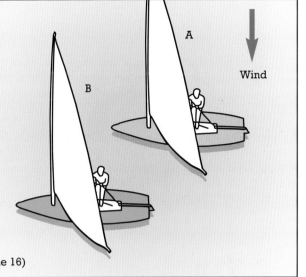

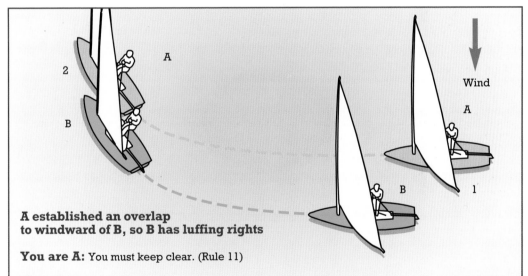

A established an overlap to windward of B, so B has luffing rights

You are A: You must keep clear. (Rule 11)

You are B: You may luff or bear away as you please provided you give A room to keep clear. (Rule 16)

The 'lock-up' position:
• At position 2, if A luffs, his stern will swing into B. If he bears away their courses will converge and there will be contact almost immediately. The only way in which A can fulfil his obligation to keep clear is to sail straight on. B can luff no more, for to do so would not be giving A room to keep clear. B may continue sailing straight ahead, or he may bear away. (Rules 11 & 16).

• It is for this reason that luffing a boat to windward is rarely worthwhile in fleet racing. B would be wise to luff to clear his wind before A gets an overlap to windward and, unless there is a port rounding mark coming up soon, encourage A to overtake to leeward.

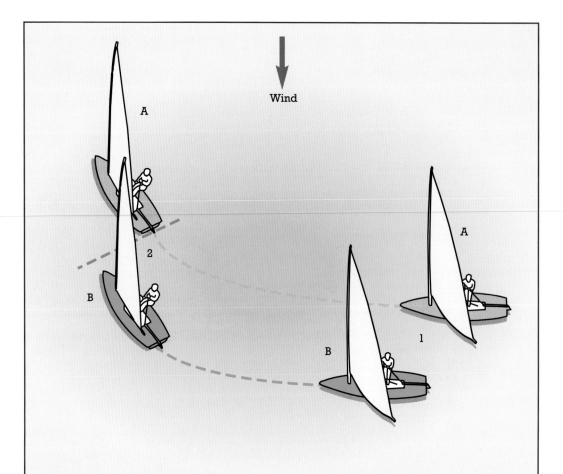

A establishes an overlap to windward of B. At position 2 the overlap is broken

You are A:
• Position 1: You established the overlap from clear astern to windward of B, so B has luffing rights. You must keep clear. (Rule 11)

• Position 2: When the overlap is broken, your only obligation is not to sail below your proper course. (Rule 17.2)

You are B:
• Position 1: You have luffing rights and may luff as high as you please but you must give A room to keep clear. (Rules 16 & 17.1)

• Position 2: When A draws ahead and the overlap is broken, you become clear astern and must therefore keep clear, but you may sail any course. (Rule 12)

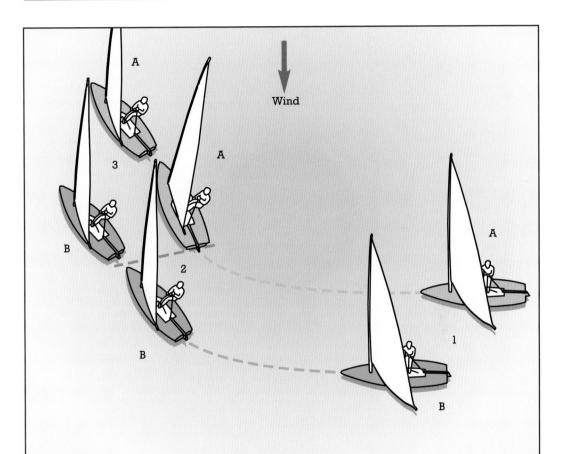

A established the overlap to windward of B

You are A:

• Position 1: You established the overlap from clear astern to windward of B, so B has luffing rights. You must keep clear. (Rule 11)

• Position 2: You can luff to break the overlap so that B becomes clear astern and must keep clear.

• Position 3: When you bear away and an overlap is re-established, B must bear away to his proper course (or lower). However, you are still the give-way boat and must keep clear. Furthermore, because it was your action that put you into a give-way position, B does not initially have to give you room to keep clear. (Rules 11 & 15)

You are B:

• Position 1: You have luffing rights and may luff as high as you please but you must give A room to keep clear. (Rule 16)

• Positions 2 & 3: When A luffs to break the overlap, and then bears away to re-establish an overlap, you lose your luffing rights. You must immediately bear away to your proper course (or lower). If to sail your proper course you need to gybe, then you must gybe. (Rule 17.1)

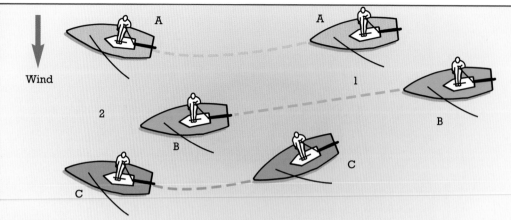

In this scenario, B establishes an overlap from clear astern to leeward of A, then while still overlapped with A, B gets an overlap to windward of C.

You are A:

• You are under no obligation to anticipate B getting an overlap, but when he does you must keep clear. Even if B does not luff, you will have to luff to avoid him running into your boom. (Rules 12 & 11)

You are B:

• When you first get an overlap to leeward of A, you must give him room to keep clear. Then you may sail up to your proper course, but no higher. (Rules 15, 16 & 17.1)

• Your proper course is the course that keeps clear of C. (Definition of 'Proper Course')

• If C luffs, you must keep clear of C who has luffing rights over both you and A, because you both established overlaps on C's windward side. (Rule 11)

You are C:

• You have luffing rights over both A and B so may luff as high as you like, but you must give them room to keep clear. (Rule 16)

Passing obstructions

You are A:

• You are the windward boat so you must keep clear of B. (Rule 11)

• If B sails to leeward of the obstruction, you may also go to leeward only if that is a proper course for you. If you do go to leeward, B must give you room, but you remain the keep-clear boat. (Rules 11, 17.2, 18.2(a))

You are B:

• If you have luffing rights, you may luff A at any time and obviously may go to windward of the obstruction. If you change course you must give A room to keep clear. (Rules 11 & 16)

• If you don't have luffing rights you may only pass to windward of the island if that is a proper course for you. Both sides are sometimes proper courses. (Rule 17.1)

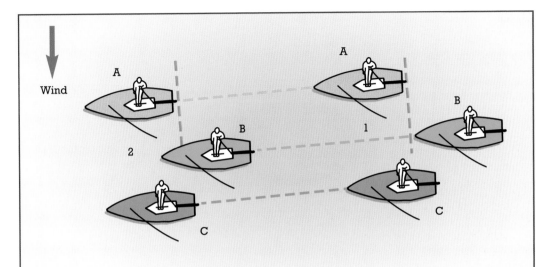

B is already overlapped with C when he gets an overlap to leeward of A.

You are B: C (the right-of-way boat) counts as a 'continuing obstruction'. When you first get the overlap between A and the continuing obstruction, was there sufficient room for you to pass between them? If you freeze the picture at position 2, and the answer is 'no', you have no right to room, and if you get an overlap on A you must keep clear of both A and C. You should have sailed to leeward of C or to windward of A. (Rules 11 & 18.5)

• Whether or not you have luffing rights, if you choose to go to leeward, and A chooses to do likewise, you must give him room to pass between you and the obstruction. (Rule 18.2(a))

• If you both sail to leeward of the obstruction, once the island has been passed, if you have luffing rights you may luff above your proper course, but you must give A room to keep clear. (Rule 16)

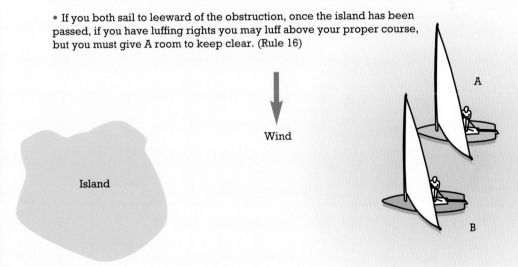

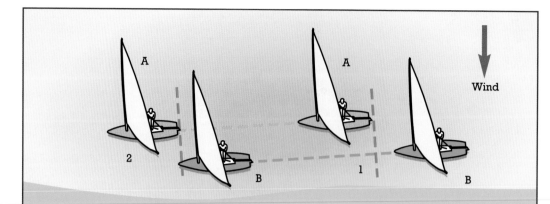

Continuing obstruction (e.g. river bank)

In position 1, B is about to get an overlap between A and the continuing obstruction.

Just as in the situation at the top of page 55, at the moment the overlap is established there is insufficient room for B to pass between A and the continuing obstruction, so B has no right to room and if he gets an overlap he must keep clear of A. (Rule 18.5)

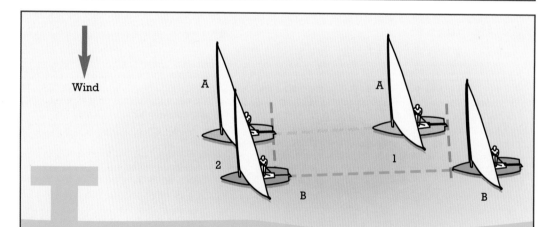

Continuing obstruction (e.g. river bank)

In position 1, B is about to get an overlap between A and the continuing obstruction.

Unlike the situation at the top of the page, at the moment the overlap is established there is sufficient room for B to pass between A and the continuing obstruction, so B has the right to room. (Rule 18.5)

At position 2, A will need to luff to give room to B to get round the jetty. (Rules 18.5 & 18.2(a))

9 Rounding the Wing Mark

When the inside boat has to gybe to sail his proper course

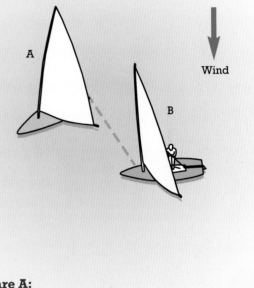

Boat B has an undisputed overlap when the leading boat reaches the two-length zone. They will be gybing round the mark.

You are A:
• B has an overlap when you reach the two-length zone, and you are the give-way boat, so you must keep clear and give room. (Rules 11 & 18.2(a))

• If you now get clear ahead, you must continue to give room until B has rounded or passed the mark (that is, left it astern). You might do this by staying ahead, but if B is forced to change course to avoid you before he has left the mark astern, you will have broken a rule. (Rule 18.2(b))

You are B:
• Even if you have luffing rights, (for example if you were more than two lengths away from A when you became overlapped, or because A got an overlap on your windward side) then because your proper course is to gybe, as soon as you are 'about to round or pass' the mark (which is usually about three boat lengths), you must sail no higher than your proper course until you have completed your gybe. (Rule 18.4)

• As A is overlapped outside you, you must gybe no later than you would have done had A not been there. (If it's very windy and you want to do a loop and tack instead of gybing, you will have to slow down and let A go ahead.) (Rule 18.4)

• After you have both gybed round the mark, and the mark is 'passed' (left clear astern with no chance of hitting it), then if you are overlapped you will be the windward boat, and you must keep clear of A. A will have luffing rights if there was an overlap when you have both gybed. (Rule 11)

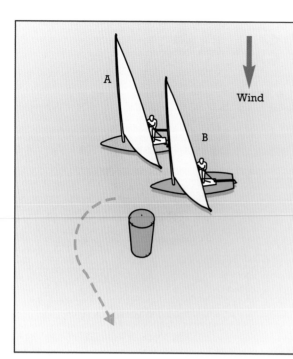

How much room must A give?

A is to windward and is, therefore, the give-way boat and must keep clear. A must also give room for B to round in a seamanlike way. B must sail a course no higher than his proper course. To comply with that obligation, B will have to gybe. If A believes B has sailed too wide (i.e. above his proper course), he can protest, but he'd be wise to keep clear, because if there is contact and the protest committee is in doubt about B's proper course, it is likely to give B the benefit of the doubt. (Rules: Definition of 'Room', 18.2. 18.4, 11)

When the inside boat does not have to gybe to sail his proper course

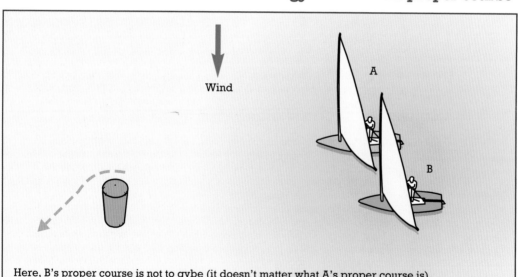

Here, B's proper course is not to gybe (it doesn't matter what A's proper course is). If B has luffing rights (usually because A established the overlap to windward of B) then B may sail straight on past the mark, or luff at any time. If B luffs, he must give room to A to keep clear.

A must give room and keep clear. If B does not have luffing rights, he may sail his proper course, but no higher, as he approaches, as he passes, and after he has passed the mark. (Rules 18.2(a), 11, 16, 17.1)

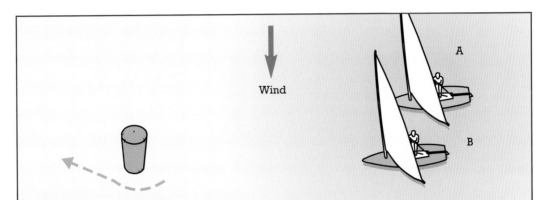

Here A, the give-way boat, will be on the inside. As soon as the boats are 'about to pass' the mark, B must start giving room, whether or not he has luffing rights. Room is 'the space a boat needs in the existing conditions while manoeuvring promptly in a seamanlike way'. A must keep clear of B.

When both boats have passed the mark (left it astern with no risk of hitting it), B may return to his proper course or, if he has luffing rights, may sail as high as he likes, but if he luffs he must give A room to keep clear. (Rules 18.2(a), 11, 16, 17.1)

When there is doubt about the overlap

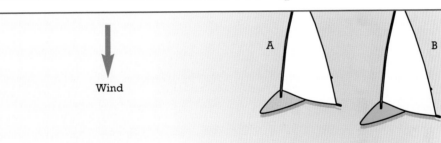

Often there is doubt whether or not there is an overlap at that critical moment when the leading boat reaches the two-length zone. It is easy to draw a picture in a book, or place models carefully on the protest room table, but in real life the moment passes in an instant. If you are flying a spinnaker and you're preparing for a gybe you'll be reluctant to spare anyone to go to the bow or stern to see if there's an overlap. In addition to knowing whether the boats are overlapped, it is difficult to judge when the leading boat is two hull lengths from the mark. Before you know it, the moment is gone, and the boats are converging towards the mark with the crew of one boat shouting 'no room' and the crew from the other shouting 'water', plus a fair number of unprintable words and phrases to give emphasis to their respective opinions.

In this diagram, who can say without the use of measuring instruments whether B has an overlap, and whether A is two lengths from the mark? If A luffs a little at the critical moment as he is just about to get to the two-length zone, maybe he could break an overlap. If this was happening on the water with boats that are moving rather than being frozen in a picture, and the overlap is in doubt, then the answer to the question 'must A give room to B?' depends on what was happening before they got to this position: see the next two diagrams.

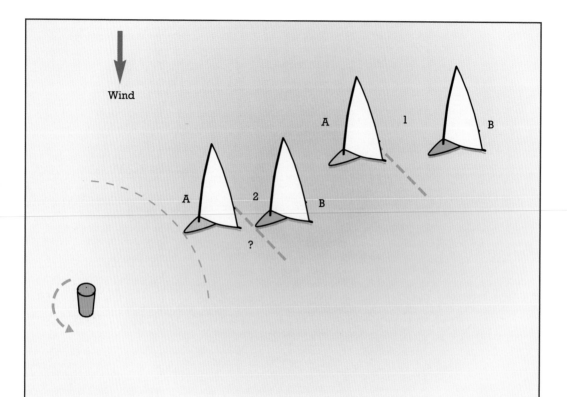

At position 1 there is no doubt that A is clear ahead. So at position 2, when there is doubt, it is resolved in A's favour. If B surges forward on a wave, A should keep clear and protest. If the water is flat, A could hail something like 'no water' and hold his proper course for the mark. B would be wise to slow down and follow A. There is no obligation on A to give room just because B is claiming he has the right to room. On the other hand, both boats are, of course, required to try to avoid contact. (Rules 18.2(e) & 14)

You are A:

Unless it is obvious that there is no overlap and B will not get one, hail 'no overlap' long before you get to the critical 'two-lengths' position, and try to get a response from B. If B subsequently claims that he got an inside overlap before the two-length zone, any doubt will be resolved in your favour. (Rules 18.2(c) & (e))

Your hail does not in itself place any obligation on B but will usually avoid a disagreement, a protest and, sometimes, damage.

seamanlike way'. This usually means you will have to begin to bear away before you get to the critical two-length zone. As soon as the boats are 'about to pass' the mark you must start giving room, whether or not you have luffing rights. (Rule 18.2(a))

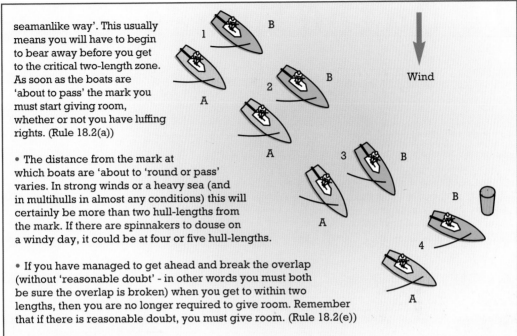

• The distance from the mark at which boats are 'about to 'round or pass' varies. In strong winds or a heavy sea (and in multihulls in almost any conditions) this will certainly be more than two hull-lengths from the mark. If there are spinnakers to douse on a windy day, it could be at four or five hull-lengths.

• If you have managed to get ahead and break the overlap (without 'reasonable doubt' - in other words you must both be sure the overlap is broken) when you get to within two lengths, then you are no longer required to give room. Remember that if there is reasonable doubt, you must give room. (Rule 18.2(e))

• From a tactical point of view, it may be better to slow down, let B go ahead, and tighten up round the mark immediately behind B, to prevent yourself getting trapped down to leeward of him as you come away from the mark. However, bear in mind that once B breaks the overlap, he is no longer limited to rounding in a 'seamanlike manner', and may sail wide and come up hard on the mark.

• If you are still overlapped when the mark is passed (left astern with no risk of hitting it), you may return to your proper course or, if you have luffing rights, may sail as high as you like, but you must give B room to keep clear. (Rule 16)

You are B:
• As you approach the mark, your obligation is to keep clear of A. (Rule 11)

• If A has luffing rights, he may luff you to windward of the mark, but he must stay outside a distance in which either of you would be 'about to round or pass' the mark. (Rule 18.1)

• When you are 'about to round or pass' the mark, you have the right to room to round inside A. Although 'room' does not mean that you can sail the course you might like to sail in the absence of A (what might be called a 'tactical' rounding) don't be intimidated by A trying to squeeze you right to the mark. If there is doubt in a protest, it is likely that A would be found not to have given sufficient room. If he doesn't give you enough room, it makes no difference whether you collide with the mark or the boat; whatever you hit (or if you hit both or even neither), if you feel you weren't given sufficient room, protest and sail on. (Rules 18.2(a), 28.1 & 31.3)

• Although A must give room, you remain the give-way boat and you must keep clear. When you have passed the mark (left it astern), A may luff to close-hauled (or his proper course if the next leg is a reach) and if he has luffing rights (can you remember how the overlap was established on the last leg?) A may luff and you must keep clear. (Rule 11)

When there is doubt about the overlap
See pages 60 and 61. The same principles apply here.

11 On the Run

All of Chapter 8 (On the Reach) applies equally on the run, but there are some additional situations which relate to boats on opposite tacks, and when one or both gybe.

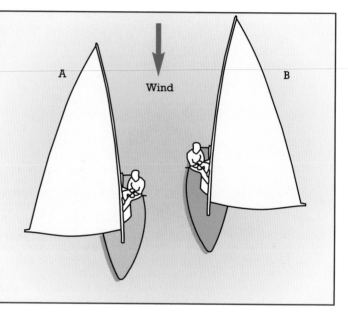

You are A:
You are on opposite tacks and you are on port tack so your obligation is simple: to keep clear of B. (Rule 10)

You are B:
You have the right to sail where you like (your proper course is irrelevant) but if you change course you must give A room to keep clear. (Rule 16)

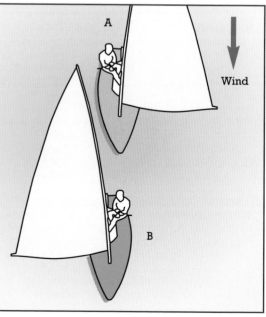

You are A:
You have the right to sail where you like (your proper course is irrelevant) but if you change course you must give B room to keep clear. (Rule 16)

You are B:
Your obligation is simple: to keep clear of A. If A is astern and going faster you'll need to do something. You could gybe on to starboard tack and become the right-of-way boat, or move out of the way. (Rule 10)

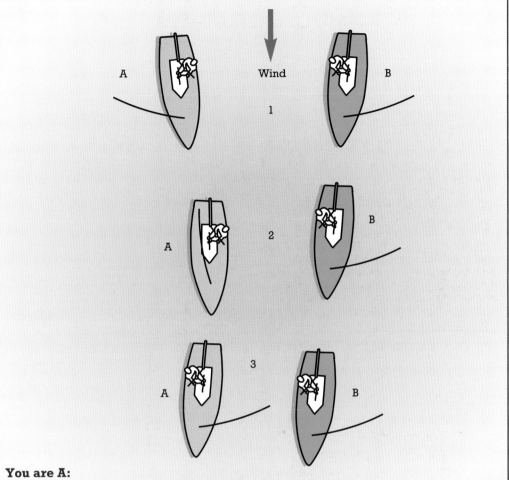

You are A:

• At position 1 you're on port tack and must keep clear. (Rule 10)

• At position 2 you are gybing into a 'give-way' position and your obligation to keep clear continues. (Rule 11)

• At position 3 you are windward boat and still required to keep clear. (Rule 11)

You are B:

• In position 1 you are the right-of-way boat, and may sail any course, but if you change course you must give A room to keep clear. (Rules 10 and 16)

• While A is gybing at position 2, you continue to be right-of-way boat, but if you change course you must give A room to keep clear. (Rules 10, 11 and 16)

• You have luffing rights as soon as A's mainsail fills on the new side, so you may continue to sail any course, but if you change course you must give A room to keep clear. (Rules 11 and 16)

In short, you are the right of way boat throughout, but if you change course you must give A room to keep clear. (Rules 10, 11 and 16)

You are A:

• At position 1 you're the right-of-way boat and may luff up to your proper course. If you've got luffing rights, you may luff as high as you like provided you give B room to keep clear. (Rules 11, 16 and 17.1)

• As soon as B's mainsail flips to fill on the port side (which means he's on starboard tack) you become the give-way boat and if you are on a collision course, as you are in position 2, you must do something to keep clear. (Rule 10)

You are B:

• At position 1 you are windward boat so you must keep clear. (Rule 11).

• From the moment you gybe you become the right-of-way boat, but you must gybe into a position which initially gives A room to keep clear, and if you change course you must give A room to keep clear. (Rules 15 & 16)

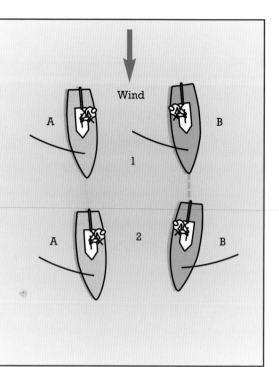

You are A:

• In position 1 you are the right-of-way boat, and may sail up to your proper course if you don't have luffing rights, and as high as you like if you do, but if you change course you must give B room to keep clear. (Rules 11 and 16)

• At position 2 you have gybed without changing course and you continue to be the right-of-way boat. As you did not change course you were not required to give B room to keep clear, but as I explained in Chapter 1, everyone must avoid contact if reasonably possible, so if your boom is going to make contact with B's boom, you should restrain it and protest. However, if there is contact with no damage, you cannot be penalised. (Rule 14)

You are B:

• At position 1 you're to windward and must keep clear. (Rule 11)

• It is wise to leave sufficient room for A to gybe, because if he does, you'll continue to be the give-way boat and he doesn't have to give you room to keep clear. (Rules 10 & 15)

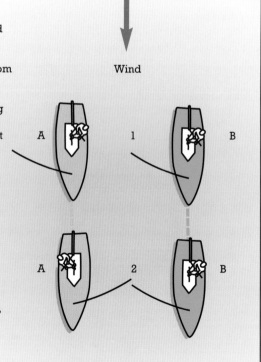

You are A:
• At position 1 you're the right-of-way boat, (you are on starboard tack), but if you change course you must give B room to keep clear. (Rules 10 & 16)

• At position 2 when B gybes you become the give-way boat and must keep clear. (Rule 11)

You are B:
• In position 1 you are the give-way boat, and must keep clear. (Rule 10)

• At position 2, when you gybe, you become the right-of-way boat, but A doesn't have to anticipate your being there, and there must be room for him to keep clear when you complete your gybe. (Rule 15)

• You may sail any course (you have luffing rights) but if you change course, you must give A room to keep clear. (Rule 16)

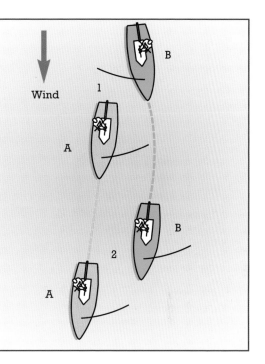

Passing a continuing obstruction

You are A:
You are on starboard tack, and B is on port tack, and you are gaining on him.

• If there is not room for you to pass between B and the continuing obstruction, and you poke your nose in, you'll become the 'keep clear' boat. (Rule 18.5)

• If there is room for you to pass between B and the continuing obstruction at the moment you get an inside overlap, then you may sail between B and the shore and you remain the right-of-way boat. (Rules 10 & 18.5)

• If you approach B's stern then B must keep clear and the only way to keep clear is to sail away from the shore. (Rule 10)

You are B:
• If there is room for A to pass between you and the continuing obstruction, then you remain the give-way boat and must keep clear, whether or not A is overlapped. This is true even if your draft is greater than A's and you can't get closer to the shore. (Rules 10 and 18.5)

• If A approaches your transom, you must keep clear. But if you gybe you become the right-of-way boat. (Rules 10 & 15)

• Your best plan is to gybe!

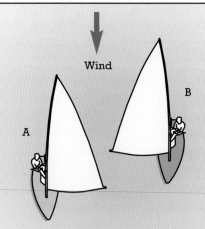

You are A:
• Your proper course is irrelevant. You may change course towards B, but only in such a way that B is able to keep clear. (Rule 16)

• Once B cannot, with safety, get any closer to the shore, then you must give him room to sail along between you and the shore. (Rule 18.2(a))

• If something sticks out from the shore ahead of B, you'll have to sail out to give B room to pass round it. (Rule 18.2(a))

• If B gybes, you become the windward boat and must keep clear. (Rule 11)

You are B:
• You must keep clear. When you cannot safely get any closer to the shore, then you may sail along the shoreline (or, more exactly, along the line that is safely close to the shore); A must give you room to do that. (Rules 10 & 18.2(a))

• There is no requirement to hail if you think he is pushing you too close for safety, but there is no other way he is to know that you think things are getting unsafe, so hail for room when you need it.

• If there is a danger projecting from the shore ahead (or if you think there is) A must give you room to come out round it; again it is advisable, though not essential, to hail for room. (Rule 18.2(a))

• If you gybe (looks like a good idea!), you become the right-of-way boat with luffing rights so you may luff above your proper course if you want to, but if you change course you must give A room to keep clear. (Rules 11 and 16)

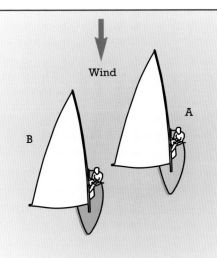

You are A:

• You must keep clear. When you cannot safely get any closer to the shore, then you may sail along the shoreline (or, more exactly, along the line that is safely close to the shore); B must give you room to do that. (Rules 11 & 18.2(a))

• There is no requirement to hail if you think he is pushing you too close for safety, but there is no other way he is to know that you think things are getting unsafe, so hail for room when you need it.

• If there is a danger projecting from the shore ahead (or if you think there is) B must give you room to come out round it; again it is advisable though not essential to hail for room. (Rule 18.2(a))

You are B:

• If you have luffing rights and A is some distance from the shore or obstruction, you may luff, but if you change course you must give him room to keep clear. (Rules 11 and 16)

• When the shore (or other obstruction) impedes A's ability to respond then you must stop luffing and bear away as is necessary to give him room. If he needs more room to come out round a projection, then you must give him room to do so. (Rule 18.2(a))

• If you don't have luffing rights, you may luff (in such a way that A can keep clear), up to your proper course. If your proper course is close to the shore, then you may force A towards the shore but must give A room when he gets there, as described in the last paragraph. (Rule 18.2(a))

12 Rounding the Leeward Mark from the Run

When the mark is a long way off, A, on port tack, would have to keep clear of B on starboard tack. On the other hand, if they were close to the mark, A has the right to room to round or pass the mark. The mark-rounding rules come into effect when the boats are 'about to round or pass' the mark. Under normal conditions, boats will have reached the 'about to round or pass' position at two hull lengths at the latest. When boats are lowering spinnakers in windy conditions with a tidal stream under them, they may be 'about to round or pass' at six or more hull lengths. On a river when boats are hardly making way against an adverse current, they may not be about to round or pass till they are less than two hull lengths from the mark.

At position 1, the boats are just reaching that critical position when they may be 'about to round or pass' the mark:

You are A:
* At position 1, you are on port tack so you must keep clear. In this situation you have little choice but to gybe. If you think you are about to round or pass, it would be best to shout this claim to B as he approaches. If he doesn't begin to give you room, keep clear and protest. (Rules 10, 18.1 & 18.2(a))

* At position 2 when you complete your gybe you are overlapped, so B has luffing rights, and you must keep clear. If you are not 'about to round or pass', he can sail you as far as he likes the wrong side of the mark. If you are 'about to round or pass the mark' then B must give you room. If you think you are 'about to round or pass', keep clear and protest. (Rules 11, 18.1 & 18.2(a))

* If you break the overlap (you could luff at position 2) then you become the right-of-way boat, but you can't just gybe in front of B, because as soon as you bear away you'll establish an overlap and be windward boat. (Rule 11)

* If after luffing to break the overlap at position 2, you bear away so that B is overlapped again, he doesn't have luffing rights and must not sail higher than his proper course. His proper course (the course he would sail if you weren't there) would be to gybe, so he must gybe. (Rule 17.1)

* If either of you get close enough to the mark that you are 'about to round or pass' then B must give you room. Room will include the space for two gybes. (Rule 18.2(a))

You are B:

• Position 1: Not to begin to give room at this position when A is claiming room leaves you open to protest and possible disqualification. If you are really going to take A the wrong side of the mark (rarely a good tactic when other boats are going to overtake you both), there has to be no doubt that you are not 'about to round or pass the mark'. But if these were Lasers on flat water with no tidal stream, you'd not be 'about to round or pass' at position 1. (Rule 18.1)

• If there is no doubt that you are not 'about to round or pass' the mark, then you may sail any course, but if you change course you must give A room to keep clear. (Rules 10 & 16)

• When A gybes at position 2, nothing changes. If there is no doubt that you are not 'about to round or pass' the mark, then you may sail any course, but if you change course you must give A room to keep clear. (Rules 11 & 16)

• If the overlap is broken at position 3 you become the give-way boat, but you may sail any course. (Rule 12)

• If the overlap is re-established, although you are the right-of-way boat, you must sail no higher than your proper course, gybing if necessary. (Rule 17.1)

Now let's go back to the approach, and assume the boats are 'about to round or pass' the mark.

You are A:

• At position 1, you are overlapping on the inside. Even though you have not yet reached the two-length zone, B may have to start giving you room. (Rule 18.2(a))

• You must keep clear of B, while B gybes (Rule 10)

• At position 3, even though you are the right-of-way boat with luffing rights, you may not sail B past the mark. You must gybe no later than the position at which you would have gybed to sail your proper course round the mark in the absence of B. B must give you room to gybe. (Rules 18.2(a) & 18.4).

• When you have gybed, if you are still overlapped as you are in position 4, you become the give-way boat and must keep clear of B, but B must give you room to round the mark. (Rules 11 & 18.2(a))

• When you have left the mark astern, then if you are still overlapped, you must continue to keep clear. B has luffing rights and may sail higher than his close-hauled course. (Rules 11, 18.1 & 18.2(a))

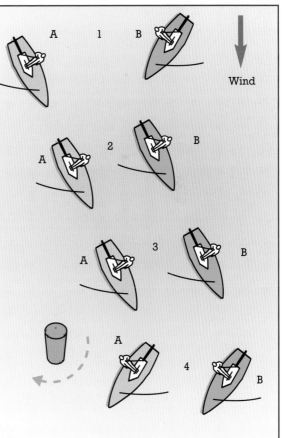

You are B:

• Position 1: Because A has an overlap as you become 'about to round or pass' the mark, you may have to start giving room before you reach the two-length zone. In this diagram, you will need to gybe at position 1. (Rule 18.2(a))

• At position 2, you become the give-way boat and you must keep clear. (Rule 11)

• A must not sail above his proper course, so at position 4 he must gybe. If he doesn't, you may protest, but you should still keep clear. (Rule 11)

• When A gybes at position 4, and you gybe, you become the right-of-way boat with luffing rights, but you must give room to A to round the mark in a seamanlike way. If he fails to keep clear, it is best to avoid contact and protest. Then you can't lose the protest: if the protest committee finds he didn't keep clear, he'll be disqualified, and if it finds he did, neither boat will be penalised. (Rule 18.2(a))

• Soon after position 4, it is best to drop astern and round up tight to the mark, rather than be left in A's windshadow. However, if you are still overlapped when both boats have completed the rounding (that is, left the mark astern), then as you have luffing rights you may luff as high as you like, but if you luff you must give A room to keep clear. (Rules 11 & 16)

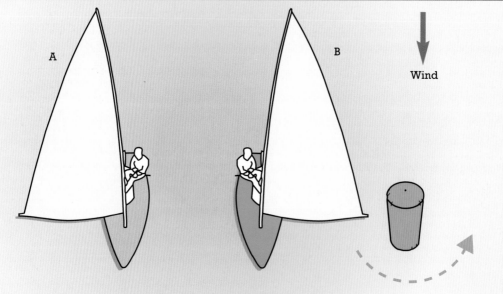

You are A:
• You must keep clear of B. (Rule 10)

• B must not sail above his proper course, so he must gybe. If he doesn't, it's best to continue to keep clear, and protest. (Rules 10 & 18.4)

You are B:
• Until you were 'about to round or pass the mark', you could sail where you liked, but if you changed course you had to give A room to keep clear. (Rule 16)

• Now you are 'about to round or pass the mark' you must sail no higher than your proper course. This will mean gybing of course (you can't sail straight on even though you are on starboard tack and A is on port tack). (Rule 18.4)

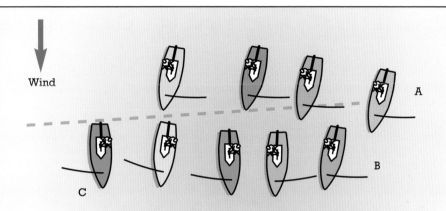

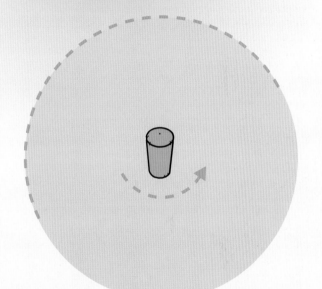

You are A:

• Although you may be able to get an overlap inside B before anyone reaches the two-length zone, there is no way B is going to be able to keep clear so that you can sail inside at the mark. Remember B is not required to anticipate your getting the overlap. Therefore you have no right to room. (Rules 11, 15 and 18.2(c) & (e))

• You do have an overlap, without doubt, on the inside of C and, unlike B, C is able to give room. C therefore must keep clear if you maintain the overlap to the two hull-lengths zone. (Rules 18.2(a) & 10)

You are B:

• As you've had the overlap for some time, those boats outside must keep clear (either because they are to windward on the same tack, or are on port tack). It might be a good idea to tell A that it's too late for him to get an overlap now. (Rules 10, 11 & 18.2(a))

• If the outside boats don't keep clear, try to get the correct side of the mark, even if it means colliding with the mark or the boat outside you (providing there is no chance of damage). If you are forced the wrong side of the mark you might succeed with a protest but you cannot recover the places lost. (Rules 62.1(b), 64.1(b) & 14)

• As you need to gybe around this mark, you mustn't sail above your proper course. But that means you may make a 'tactical rounding'. (Rule 18.4)

You are C:

• This is not a good place to be! A has an inside overlap, and you are able to keep clear, so keep clear you must, as well as keeping clear of all the boats inside you. Next time, don't get into this position! (Rules 10 & 18.2(a))

13 The Finish

You finish when any part of your hull, crew or equipment first touches the finishing line, from the direction of the last mark. Typically, the first part of the boat to cross the line is the stem, but your crew's hand held over his head when he's out on the trapeze would count if that was his 'normal position'.

With a downwind finish, the spinnaker is usually the first piece of equipment to cross the line. If the spinnaker head was let out a few centimetres, and the boat often sailed with it like that, that would be OK, but a spinnaker with its head let go several metres would not count, because it would not be in its normal position (whether this had been done intentionally or not). A boat that had let its spinnaker go would be finished on the first piece of the boat to cross the line that was not out of position - probably its stem or pulpit.

You are 'racing' until you have cleared the finishing line and the finishing marks, having completed any penalty turns for hitting a finishing mark or exonerating yourself for breaking a rule in relation to another boat. You have cleared the line when no part of your boat or its equipment is straddling the line. You have cleared the finishing marks when you are first in a position that is not in danger of making contact with a mark. The usual way of doing this is just to keep sailing right over the line near the middle (which would mean you are clear of the marks) or, if you finish near an end, to sail right through the line and get clear of the mark.

You don't have to cross the line completely; having finished with the first part of the boat or its equipment touching the line, you can duck back on to the course side of the line if you want to.

When you have finished and cleared the line, you are still subject to the racing rules, but you cannot be penalised (so there is no need to take a penalty) for infringing a 'when boats meet' rule (unless you interfere with a boat that is still racing). (Rules: Part 2 Preamble and 22.1)

If you have not sailed the correct course, even after finishing you can go back and complete the course.

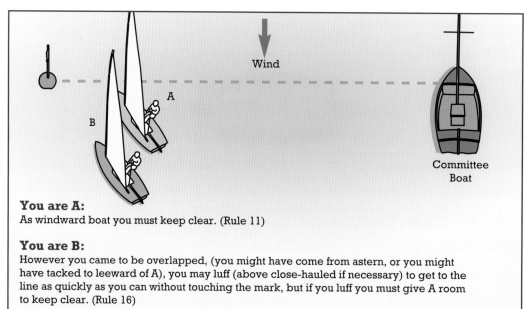

Wind

Committee Boat

You are A:
As windward boat you must keep clear. (Rule 11)

You are B:
However you came to be overlapped, (you might have come from astern, or you might have tacked to leeward of A), you may luff (above close-hauled if necessary) to get to the line as quickly as you can without touching the mark, but if you luff you must give A room to keep clear. (Rule 16)

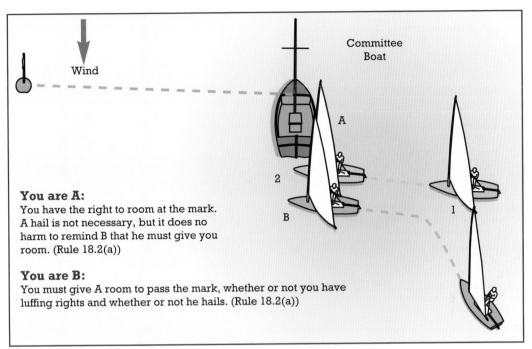

You are A:
You have the right to room at the mark.
A hail is not necessary, but it does no
harm to remind B that he must give you
room. (Rule 18.2(a))

You are B:
You must give A room to pass the mark, whether or not you have
luffing rights and whether or not he hails. (Rule 18.2(a))

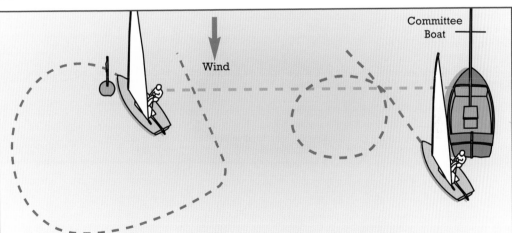

If, before finishing, you touch a finishing mark (a buoy or the committee boat) you must sail
clear of other boats and do a turn penalty including a tack and a gybe (it doesn't matter which
comes first). You must then sail to where you are wholly on the course side of the line, and
finish. (Rule 31.2)

If you hit the mark after finishing but before clearing the line and the mark, you 'unfinish'
yourself when you hit it. You must sail clear of other boats and do a 360 penalty, sail to where
you are wholly on the course side of the line, and then finish again. (Rule 31.2)

You don't have to be clear of the line when you do the 360 (you can be straddling it or on the
post-finish side of it), but if, having taken the penalty, you are not on the course side, you must
go back to the course side, and then finish. (Rule 31.2)

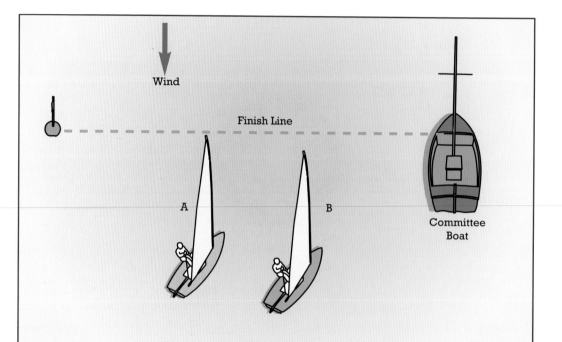

You are A:

As windward boat you must keep clear of B, even if B luffs. Whether or not he has luffing rights, B has the right to luff to head-to-wind to finish as quickly as he can. (Rules 11, 17.1 definition of 'proper course')

If B hails for room to tack, you have to make a quick judgement as to whether you can fetch the committee boat on this tack. To 'fetch' means to pass without tacking, so you can luff to head-to-wind but you must get past the bow of the committee boat without going through head-to-wind. If you can, you can refuse room (you should hail a refusal such as 'no room') but if you refuse room and then cannot fetch the committee boat, you'll have to do a 720-degree penalty before you can be recorded as having finished. (Rule 19.2)

If you cannot lay the committee boat, you must either:

1. Tack, or

2. Hail back 'you tack' and take on the responsibility of giving room to B (typically by ducking B's stern as he tacks).

You are B:

Because of the obstruction ahead, you may hail A for room to tack. If A refuses to tack or otherwise give room, you may 'shoot' the line; that is, sail head-to-wind and hope you will have sufficient way for your bow to touch the line - that's all you need! If A refuses to respond to your hail, slow and tack under his stern. If he fails to fetch the committee boat without tacking, you may protest him if he doesn't take a penalty. (Rule 19)

If A responds to your hail by tacking, you must tack as soon as possible. (Rule 19.1(a))

If A responds to your hail by hailing 'you tack', you must tack. (Rule 19.1(b))

14 Means of Propulsion

You must not 'increase, maintain or decrease' the speed of your boat by any means other than by using 'wind and water'. At major dinghy championships the sailing instructions often allow the jury to penalise boats it sees infringing the propulsion rule, without a hearing. Often, jury members go afloat and protest boats they believe are breaking the rule. (Rules 42 & 67)

The differential in speed between a dinghy complying with the propulsion rule and one propelled illegally by a skilled crew paying no attention to it can, in very light winds, be so enormous that in a half-knot zephyr the complying boat wouldn't have reached the windward mark when the infringing boat had completed the course, travelling six times as fast. (Rule 42)

The difference lessens as the wind speed increases, but can still be significant in a competitive fleet at a wind speed of 10 knots. Since the difference in boatspeed between top competitors in competitive dinghy fleets is often as little as one tenth of one per cent, breaking Rule 42 is an obvious attraction not only to the unscrupulous, but to the honest sailor when he sees less honest sailors 'getting away with it'.

So what does Rule 42 seek to control? If you rock a rig to windward in still air, the sail passing through the still air has the same effect as moving air passing over a still sail: a driving force is set up. The same sort of effect, though not quite as effective, can be obtained by hauling in the sail: the force drives the boat forward, and the rig or sail can be returned to 'leeward' ready for another go. Waggling the tiller can also drive a hull through calm water. Moving the trunk of the body forward and backwards, even in strong winds, can flap the leech and increase the sail's drive.

With practice one can become very efficient at driving a boat through the water on a calm day; it's really quite fun, though very energetic. There is a minority of dinghy sailors who would prefer that there were no restrictions (i.e. most of the prohibitions in Rule 42 were removed as they are for boardsailing (see Appendix B)). Removing the propulsion restrictions would certainly make life easier for race committees and juries, since the rule is not easy to enforce. However, the vast majority of good sailors do not want 'kinetics' (imparting energy from moving crew weight into forward motion) to be part of sailing. Attitudes might change; up to a few years ago, board sailors did not want to allow kinetics, now they do, resulting in only very fit and strong people being able to win boardsailing championships.

At championships, and at well-organised regional regattas, a jury goes afloat to look for offenders; a good race committee will also not hesitate to take action. However, this should not change your policy; if you see someone pumping, rocking or sculling, you should protest, and not break the rule yourself.

Some classes have a rule that allows the Race Committee to display a flag when the wind is at, say, 10 knots or more. The pumping and rocking prohibitions are then suspended, to the joy of sailors and judges.

15 Taking a Penalty

When and where to take a penalty

When you know you've broken a rule or a sailing instruction, you must take a penalty or retire promptly from the race, unless the rule or sailing instruction broken is one which requires you do something while racing, and you were not racing at the time of the incident (i.e. it occurred before the preparatory signal or after you finish and clear the finishing line). In such a case you do not have to take a penalty (but if you've caused damage you may have to pay for the repair).

If you are racing and you break a 'when boats meet' rule, you must take a Two-Turns Penalty promptly. Let's suppose you are sailing up the first beat, and you are close-hauled on port tack, chatting to your crew about tactics. Suddenly you are aware of a starboard tack boat bearing away under your stern. As he bears away under your stern he shouts something at you so you know he is aggrieved. What should you do? Tell him you're going to take a penalty, and immediately sail clear of other boats and do a Two-Turns Penalty. Actually, if he doesn't hail 'protest' he cannot protest, but that should not affect whether or not you take the penalty. If you know you have broken a rule, and the other sailor is aggrieved, the paragraph called 'Sportsmanship and the Rules' at the beginning of the rulebook makes it clear that you must take the penalty. Not to do so could result in a protest under Rule 2 'Fair Sailing' or a report resulting in a 'Rule 69 hearing' against you for a 'gross breach of good sportsmanship'.

What if you did see him coming and when you were just about to tack, he shouted 'carry on'? You carry on on port tack and he bears away under your stern. Should you take a penalty? No. By accepting his invitation to carry on, and him ducking your stern, you have in fact kept clear. (By the way, the hail of 'carry on' did not compel you to sail on; you could have tacked if you had wanted to).

What if he bears away under your stern, but says nothing? My recommendation is that if he shows no signs of being aggrieved, then you can assume you kept clear.

If you touch a mark while racing, then you are honour-bound to take a 360-degree penalty, even if no one saw you. This is the test of a good sportsman. We all need to be good sportsmen if we are going to play this great game of fleet racing without the need for referees or judges. (Rule 31.2)

If you sail the wrong course, or propel the boat by means other than by the use of 'wind and water', or you are on the course side of the starting line at the starting signal, you cannot exonerate yourself by taking a penalty. However, you can often exonerate yourself by doing something else; if you've gone round a mark the wrong way, you can unwind yourself and go round it the right way; if you were a premature starter you can usually go back and start. But having pumped your way down the reaching leg, or paddled, or moored up to the shore for an ice-cream, or - heaven forbid - failed to rescue someone in distress, then there is no exoneration procedure open to you, and you must retire from the race immediately you realise you have broken the rule or sailing instruction.

Remember that if you want to take a Two-Turns Penalty after an incident in the preparatory period, or you hit a starting mark in the preparatory period, then you may (in fact you must) take the penalty as soon as you can, so if the infringement is some minutes before the start, you will not be disadvantaged.

If the infringement happens on or close to the finishing line, then you must do the Two-Turns Penalty as soon as possible (on either side of the finishing line or its extensions), get your boat wholly on the course side of the line, and then cross the finishing line in the direction from the last mark. It is possible, therefore, to finish (when the first part of the boat touches the line), then break a rule of Part 2 before clearing the line (which has the effect of 'un-finishing'), do a Two-Turns Penalty, then come back wholly behind the line and 'refinish' when the first part of the boat touches the line again from the course side.

If you break a 'when boats meet' rule (for example by taking room at a mark to which you are not entitled) and you hit the mark, you can exonerate yourself by doing just a Two-Turns Penalty; you don't have to do the one-turn penalty for hitting the mark as well. If you have broken more than one rule in an incident, you need take only one Two-Turns Penalty.

How to take the penalty

The standard penalty for infringing a 'when boats meet' rule is the 'Two-Turns Penalty', which is described in Rule 44.2. If there is nothing said about penalties in the sailing instructions, then the Two-Turns Penalty applies.

If you have room, do the penalty immediately (and it costs you nothing to tell the other sailor you're going to do it). If there isn't room, tell the other sailor you're going to do it, immediately sail to where there is room, or slow down to let the surrounding boats pass. Rotate your boat through two turns and include two tacks and two gybes. When you are training, you should practise doing Two-Turns Penalties so that you can do them as quickly as possible; there's no point in adding to the penalising effect by getting into irons. When you're on a beat, it's usually best to bear off first rather than tack. (Rule 44.2)

Sometimes sailing instructions replace the

'Two-Turns Penalty' with a 'scoring' penalty system (usually for keelboat events in which it is thought unsafe for boats to be doing circles, or because they have different ratings). When the sailing instructions prescribe a 'scoring penalty' then instead of doing a Two-Turns Penalty, you must display a yellow flag and inform the race committee after the finish that you are taking a penalty. (Rule 44.3)

Protest, take a penalty, or both?

After the preparatory signal, if you are involved in an incident with another boat (or several other boats) in which you think a rule has, or may have, been broken, you have to make a decision and you have to make it quickly. If there has been a collision, however small or unavoidable, then almost certainly a rule will have been broken, and of course even without a collision there might have been an infringement.

If you know you have broken a rule but think the other boat has broken one too, you can protest and take a penalty. Hail 'protest', then sail clear and take the Two-Turns Penalty.

If you have a collision or touch a mark, but were in the right or entitled to room, and there is no damage then you cannot be penalised. You can sail on. If there is damage (to either boat) which you could have avoided then you can do a Two-Turns Penalty to exonerate yourself. If the damage is serious, then you cannot exonerate yourself with a Two-Turns Penalty, and you must retire.

16 Protesting

Some people, even very experienced competitors, say they find protesting unpleasant. Protesting need not be done with any acrimony whatsoever, and unless we want to evolve a breed of referees to blow whistles and penalise on the spot (and there'll need to be lots of them all over the course, because under such a system no one will consider taking a penalty if they don't hear a whistle) then we have to accept that the sport is policed by the following system:

When a competitor knows he has broken a rule he takes a penalty (or retires) whether or not the other sailor hails 'protest'.

When a competitor thinks another competitor has broken a rule, and the other competitor doesn't retire or take a penalty, he protests.

When the race committee (or jury if there is one) sees a rule infringement which affects the fairness of the competition and the boat doesn't take a penalty, it protests.

In my opinion (though many judges will not agree with me) there is one other consideration that affects a decision as to whether or not a penalty should be taken or a protest made against another boat when a rule is broken. That is, whether or not the right-of-way boat (or the boat with the right to room) is aggrieved. You're on starboard tack a lap ahead of a beginner on port tack and you have to duck under his stern. There is nothing to be gained by protesting; a word over a beer after the race would be much more appropriate. Of course there is no rule requiring you to protest. But what if you're the one on port tack and a rival ducks under your stern, but says nothing. As I said in the last chapter, I believe if he is not aggrieved, you can assume there's no infringement. That's the criteria I use when I'm racing. If he says even 'tut tut', I'll do a penalty if I think I've broken a rule. Sometimes I'm not sure if I have broken a rule. If the other sailor thinks I have, that's usually enough for me, and I'll go and do my turns.

When you consider another boat has broken a rule and you feel aggrieved about it, you will want to protest. This chapter is about how to lodge a protest.

There are certain requirements that must be met before a protest can be accepted as valid, and a hearing opened. The only requirement you actually need to remember is the one which has to be met out there on the water; the rest you can look up in this book when you are back at the clubhouse.

Things to remember on the water

Any boat may protest, provided that the protesting boat was involved in or witnessed an incident. Even if you have been involved in a previous incident in which you will be disqualified (after a hearing), that doesn't remove your right to protest about a later incident. (ISAF Case 1)

The important thing you need to do at the time of the incident is to hail the word 'protest'. The rule says this must be done 'at the first reasonable opportunity'. So there is time to ask him whether he's going to take a penalty, and if he says 'no', hail 'protest'. If you get no reaction to the hail, it's best to repeat it more loudly.

If your hull length is 6 metres or more, you also need to display a protest flag, and this too must be done 'at the first reasonable opportunity'. Don't wait too long. Many protests have been found to be invalid because the flag was not displayed very soon after the incident. The flag must be red. It doesn't matter what the shape is, but it must be red, and it must be a flag, not a red glove or waterproof jacket. The usual flag is the code flag B which has swallowtails, but a rectangular red flag will do just as well. It must be displayed conspicuously which means it mustn't be too small, and it must be up in the rigging and not lying on the deck. It must be kept displayed until you have finished and cleared the finishing line.

If the flag is already being displayed because of a previous incident, then that's fine; you don't have to pull it down and put it up again, or display another one.

The purpose of the hail and the flag is two-fold. It gives an opportunity for the protestee to take a penalty, and if he decides not to take a penalty, then it marks the moment so that he can recall what happened.

Remember if your hull length is less than 6 metres, you don't need to display a flag (unless the sailing instruction require it, but hopefully the practice of sailing intructions requiring a flag will soon die out).

You cannot lodge a protest if you don't hail, but you don't have to go ahead and lodge the protest if you have hailed.

If the other sailor might not have heard your hail of 'protest' at the time of the incident you should inform him again at the next opportunity you get, even if the next opportunity is ashore.

Things to do when you come ashore

You need to fill in a protest form. If you can't find one, and unless there is some special sailing instruction (ugh!) any bit of paper will do provided that you include certain pieces of vital information. Most people make too much of filling in the form. By including too much detail, you're more likely to do yourself harm than good, and you'll certainly wear out the brain unnecessarily. Initially you need only briefly describe the incident (so that the protestee can identify it), who you are, and the identity of the protestee.

You need to lodge the form with the protest committee within the time limit (which is two hours after the last boat finishes unless otherwise specified in the sailing instructions). If there is a good reason for any delay, the protest committee must extend the time limit. (Rule 61.3)

Preparing your witnesses

If there is someone who you think saw the incident, approach him and, having simply identified the incident so that he knows what you're taking about, ask him what he saw. Don't tell him anything and don't ask leading questions. If you think what he saw is what you

believe really happened, then ask him if he will be a witness at the hearing.

At the hearing, when you are invited to call witnesses, explain to the chairman that you have not discussed the case with your witness, you merely asked what he saw and considered that as this was more or less what actually happened, you thought he would be a good witness.

When your witness gives his evidence and is questioned, it will invariably become obvious to the protest committee that he has in no way been influenced, and his credibility and the value of his evidence will help you enormously. You'd do better with no witness at all than a 'coached' witness; their complicity is obvious to all but the most inexperienced protest committee.

Conducting yourself at the hearing

If you are an experienced racing skipper sailing in a minor event, there is a good chance that you will know more about the rules and procedures than the protest committee does. Use this knowledge carefully if you wish not to be disadvantaged. At any hearing you should treat the committee members (and indeed the other parties and witnesses) with respect. They are usually fellow sailors doing their best to be fair, but even when this is not the case, losing your cool gains you nothing.

The procedure

Appendix M of the racing rules, which gives a recommended procedure for protest committees, is very well written and easy to follow. Here is a summary.

The protestor and protestee are called to the hearing. You must both be present during all of the taking of evidence (from each of you, and of any witnesses called by you, by your opponent or by the protest committee). If one party chooses not to attend, then the protest committee can proceed without him.

The validity of the protest must be considered by the protest committee:

'Was a hail of "Protest" made, and was it made at the first reasonable opportunity after the incident?' For boats over 6 metres: 'Was the protest flag displayed, and was it displayed at the first reasonable opportunity after the incident?' 'Was it conspicuously displayed?' 'Was it kept displayed till the finish?'

'Was the written protest received by the race committee within the time limit?'

'If not, was there a good reason for it being received late?'

'Did the written protest identify the nature of the incident?'

Although the protest committee must extend the time limit for receiving protests if there is a good reason for a delay, it has no power to excuse any of the other requirements, and if they are not met the protest must be found to be invalid, and refused. A protest committee cannot find as a fact that the protestor did not hail 'protest' and declare "We'll let you off this time, but don't forget for next time" and proceed to hear the protest.

If the protest is ruled as valid, the protest committee must proceed to the next stage: the hearing of evidence.

The protestor describes his version of the incident; the protestee then does likewise. Each may question the other and the protest committee members may question both. Each is invited to call witnesses, one at a time, and each witness describes his version of the incident, and is questioned by the parties (the protestor and the protestee) and the committee. The committee may call witnesses, or the committee members may themselves be witnesses in which case they give their evidence and may be questioned. The protestor summarises his case; the protestee summarises his defence.

The protest committee deliberates in private (if there were observers, they too are asked to leave) and produces 'facts found' (what it thinks happened), its decision and the grounds for that decision. The parties are then recalled and the chairman reads out the details.

17 Requesting Redress & Appealing

If you think your position in a race, or in a series, has been made significantly worse through no fault of your own, you can sometimes successfully 'request redress' (often erroneously called 'protesting the race committee'). Redress is usually in the form of points that the protest committee considers you would have been awarded had you finished without being prejudiced. (Rules 62, 64.2)

Unlike a protest (for which there are several validity requirements), it is rare for a request for redress to be refused on the grounds it is invalid. The only reason for refusal to hear a redress request would be that it was received after the closing time for receiving protests (usually two hours after the incident), without a good reason.

You can write your request on any bit of paper, but is usual to use a protest form even though many of the prompts are not relevant. For example, you don't have to display a protest flag, or make a hail.

So it is not difficult to get a hearing; being awarded redress is another matter! Generally the procedure at the hearing is the same as a protest hearing, except that if you are the only one requesting redress, you will take on the 'protestor's' role, and a representative of the race committee will usually act as the 'defendant'.

The protest committee should be independent of the race committee; if you think it isn't, raise the issue early in the proceedings. If the event is anything more than a club race, wise organisers will have appointed a protest committee that is independent of the race committee; at an international event there'll usually be an international jury. At club events the usual practice is for the race committee to arrange a protest committee as independent as is practical, if a request for redress is received by the race committee.

Like a protest hearing, there are the same distinct parts to the hearing: the taking of evidence (from you, your fellow redress requesters if there are any, the race committee, and anyone else you, the race committee, or the protest committee sees fit to call); the assessment by the protest committee (sitting in private) as to whether redress is applicable; and lastly, if redress is applicable, what redress will be given.

Redress can be given to you only when:

• Your finishing position has been made significantly worse.

• You've done nothing wrong yourself. So if you have been scored 'OCS' ('on course side' for being over the line at the start), and are simply complaining that there were some boats ahead of you that were not scored OCS, you can't get redress. (You could protest the guilty boats, of course.)

• Your finishing position was affected for one of the following reasons:

(a) The race committee (or the protest committee) made an improper action or omission. So if some passing whale rammed you, you cannot get redress; a rescue boat would be another matter, as that would be under the control of the race committee. If the race committee fails to make a signal correctly and this affected you, you'd be entitled to redress. Redress can be given if there is an act or ommission of the race committee even if it adheres to the rules and sailing instructions that govern its conduct.

For example, if the race committee writes itself a sailing instruction saying it can shorten course at any time for any reason, and it shortens course for no apparent reason just as your rival approaches the first mark after twenty minutes of racing - his father is the race officer - you would have a legitimate claim for redress. Conversely, if the sailing instructions said the first leg would be 3 kilometres long and it was only 2.5, it would be impossible to argue that any competitor had been prejudiced and so no redress could be given.

(b) You have been physically damaged by a boat required to keep clear or give room or by a vessel not racing that was required to keep clear of you (for example under the collision regulations). So if you're on starboard and a boat on port rams you, putting a hole in your side, and you have to retire, you can get redress. You can only get redress if you're damaged; if you simply got tangled up with this port tacker while some close rivals pass you, you cannot get redress. If at a mark you are entitled to room but not given it and forced the wrong side, you must return to round or pass the mark correctly, and although you may successfully protest the boat that didn't give you room, because you were not physically damaged you are not entitled to redress for the fifty places you may have lost.

(c) You went to help someone in distress. If you see someone in distress you are required to go to their aid, so if you lose places by your heroic act you are entitled to redress.

(d) You have been significantly affected by someone who is penalised (under Rule 69) for cheating, or infringing the 'Fair Sailing' rule.

The protest committee will hear your evidence and that of your witnesses, and if relevant the evidence and advice of the race committee. In private it will then 'find facts' and assess whether these facts meet the criteria for giving redress, and if they do, what redress is to be given.

If your request meets the above criteria, then you must be given redress. It is not unusual to be awarded points equal to a position the protest committee thinks you would have achieved had you not been prejudiced, or points equal to your 'average to date in the series' (perhaps not counting your 'discard'). In giving redress, the only restriction imposed on the protest committee is that its decision must be as fair as possible to all boats affected. Faced with a complex situation, a protest committee may decide that the fairest arrangement is 'no adjustment to any finishing positions'. To abandon or cancel a race is rarely the fairest solution, although sometimes there is no alternative. (Rule 64.2)

Appealing

If you are penalised as a result of a hearing, you usually have the right to appeal against the protest committee's decision, but to be eligible you need to be a 'party' directly affected by the decision against which you are appealing. (Rules 70 & 71)

If you are indirectly affected, for instance, if you find yourself in a lower position as a result of the protest committee giving redress to another boat then you must first request redress on the grounds that the committee's action materially prejudiced your finishing position, and if you are not satisfied with that decision, you may appeal. You may also appeal against a decision not to hear your protest or your request for redress, or against the fairness of redress awarded as a result of your request.

Sometimes there is no right to appeal. You have no right to appeal:

• When, at an international event, an 'international jury' has been appointed, and it complies with the requirements of Appendix N; or

• When 'it is essential to determine promptly the result of a race that will qualify a boat to compete in a later stage of an event or a subsequent event'. In the UK, the approval from the Royal Yachting Association is also required. In the USA, no approval is required from the USSA. In all cases, the fact that decisions are not open to appeal must be announced in the notice of the race and in the sailing instructions. (Rules 70.4(a) & Appendix J 1.2(11))

Unless the facts found by the protest committee are completely incompatible with all the evidence or with the protest committee's own diagram, you can appeal only on a question of interpretation of the rules, and not against the facts found by the protest committee. (Rule 70.1)

The protest committee may itself refer a case it has decided for confirmation or correction. (Rule 70.2)

How to appeal

This varies from country to country, so look at Rule 70 and any prescription to the rule that your own national authority may have written.

The
RACING RULES
of SAILING
for 2005–2008

International Sailing Federation

INTRODUCTION

The Racing Rules of Sailing includes two main sections. The first, Parts 1–7, contains rules that affect all competitors. The second, Appendices A–P, provides details of rules, rules that apply to particular kinds of racing, and rules that affect only a small number of competitors or officials.

Revision The racing rules are revised and published every four years by the International Sailing Federation (ISAF), the international authority for the sport. This edition becomes effective on 1 January 2005. Marginal markings indicate important changes to Parts 1–7 and the Definitions of the 2001–2004 edition. No changes are contemplated before 2009, but any changes determined to be urgent before then will be announced through national authorities and posted on the ISAF website (www.sailing.org).

ISAF Codes The ISAF Eligibility, Advertising and Anti-Doping Codes (Regulations 19, 20 and 21) are referred to in the definition *Rule* but are not included in this book because they can be changed at any time. New versions will be announced through national authorities and posted on the ISAF website.

Cases and Calls The ISAF publishes interpretations of the racing rules in *The Case Book for 2005–2008* and recognizes them as authoritative interpretations and explanations of the rules. It also publishes *The Call Book for Match Racing for 2005–2008* and *The Call Book for Team Racing for 2005–2008*, and it recognizes them as authoritative only for umpired match or team racing. These publications are available on the ISAF website.

Terminology A term used in the sense stated in the Definitions is printed in italics or, in preambles, in bold italics (for example, *racing* and **racing**). 'Boat' means a sailboat and the crew on board. 'Race committee' includes any person or committee performing a race committee function. Other words and terms are used in the sense ordinarily understood in nautical or general use.

Appendices When the rules of an appendix apply, they take precedence over any conflicting rules in Parts 1–7. Each appendix is identified by a letter. A reference to a rule in an appendix will contain the letter and the rule number (for example, 'rule A1'). There is no Appendix I or O.

Changes to the Rules The prescriptions of a national authority, class rules or the sailing instructions may change a racing rule only as permitted in rule 86.

Changes to National Authority Prescriptions A national authority may restrict changes to its prescriptions as provided in rule 87.

BASIC PRINCIPLE

SPORTSMANSHIP AND THE RULES
Competitors in the sport of sailing are governed by a body of *rules* that they are expected to follow and enforce. A fundamental principle of sportsmanship is that when competitors break a *rule* they will promptly take a penalty, which may be to retire.

PART 1 – FUNDAMENTAL RULES

1 SAFETY
1.1 Helping Those in Danger
A boat or competitor shall give all possible help to any person or vessel in danger.

1.2 Life-Saving Equipment and Personal Buoyancy
A boat shall carry adequate life-saving equipment for all persons on board, including one item ready for immediate use, unless her class rules make some other provision. Each competitor is individually responsible for wearing personal buoyancy adequate for the conditions.

2 FAIR SAILING
A boat and her owner shall compete in compliance with recognized principles of sportsmanship and fair play. A boat may be penalized under this rule only if it is clearly established that these principles have been violated. A disqualification under this rule shall not be excluded from the boat's series score.

3 ACCEPTANCE OF THE RULES
By participating in a race conducted under these racing rules, each competitor and boat owner agrees

(a) to be governed by the *rules*;

(b) to accept the penalties imposed and other action taken under the *rules*, subject to the appeal and review procedures provided in them, as the final determination of any matter arising under the *rules*; and

(c) with respect to such determination, not to resort to any court or other tribunal not provided in the *rules*.

4 DECISION TO RACE

The responsibility for a boat's decision to participate in a race or to continue *racing* is hers alone.

5 BANNED SUBSTANCES AND METHODS

A competitor shall neither take a substance nor use a method banned by the Olympic Movement Anti-Doping Code or the World Anti-Doping Agency and shall comply with ISAF Regulation 21, Anti-Doping Code. An alleged or actual breach of this rule shall be dealt with under Regulation 21. It shall not be grounds for a *protest* and rule 63.1 does not apply.

PART 2 – WHEN BOATS MEET

*The rules of Part 2 apply between boats that are sailing in or near the racing area and intend to **race**, are **racing**, or have been **racing**. However, a boat not **racing** shall not be penalized for breaking one of these rules, except rule 22.1. When a boat sailing under these rules meets a vessel that is not, she shall comply with the International Regulations for Preventing Collisions at Sea (IRPCAS) or government right-of-way rules. However, an alleged breach of those rules shall not be grounds for a **protest** except by the race committee or protest committee. If the sailing instructions so state, the rules of Part 2 are replaced by the right-of-way rules of the IRPCAS or by government right-of-way rules.*

SECTION A
RIGHT OF WAY

*A boat has right of way when another boat is required to **keep clear** of her. However, some rules in Sections B, C and D limit the actions of a right-of-way boat.*

10 ON OPPOSITE TACKS

When boats are on opposite *tacks*, a *port-tack* boat shall *keep clear* of a *starboard-tack* boat.

11 ON THE SAME TACK, OVERLAPPED

When boats are on the same *tack* and *overlapped*, a *windward* boat shall *keep clear* of a *leeward* boat.

12 ON THE SAME TACK, NOT OVERLAPPED

When boats are on the same *tack* and not *overlapped*, a boat *clear astern* shall *keep clear* of a boat *clear ahead*.

13 WHILE TACKING

After a boat passes head to wind, she shall *keep clear* of other boats until she is on a close-hauled course. During that time rules 10, 11 and 12 do not apply. If two boats are subject to this rule at the same time, the one on the other's port side or the one astern shall *keep clear*.

SECTION B
GENERAL LIMITATIONS

14 AVOIDING CONTACT

A boat shall avoid contact with another boat if reasonably possible. However, a right-of-way boat or one entitled to *room*

(a) need not act to avoid contact until it is clear that the other boat is not *keeping clear* or giving *room*, and

(b) shall not be penalized under this rule unless there is contact that causes damage or injury.

15 ACQUIRING RIGHT OF WAY

When a boat acquires right of way, she shall initially give the other boat *room* to *keep clear*, unless she acquires right of way because of the other boat's actions.

16 CHANGING COURSE

16.1 When a right-of-way boat changes course, she shall give the other boat *room* to *keep clear*.

16.2 In addition, when after the starting signal a *port-tack* boat is *keeping clear* by sailing to pass astern of a *starboard-tack* boat, the *starboard-tack* boat shall not change course if as a result the *port-tack* boat would immediately need to change course to continue *keeping clear*.

17 ON THE SAME TACK; PROPER COURSE

17.1 If a boat *clear astern* becomes *overlapped* within two of her hull lengths to *leeward* of a boat on the same *tack*, she shall not sail above her *proper course* while they remain *overlapped* within that distance, unless in doing so she promptly sails astern of the other boat. This rule does not apply if the *overlap* begins while the *windward* boat is required by rule 13 to *keep clear*.

17.2 Except on a beat to windward, while a boat is less than two of her hull lengths from a *leeward* boat or a boat *clear astern* steering a course to *leeward* of her, she shall not sail below her *proper course* unless she gybes.

SECTION C
AT MARKS AND OBSTRUCTIONS

To the extent that a Section C rule conflicts with a rule in Section A or B, the Section C rule takes precedence.

18 ROUNDING AND PASSING MARKS AND OBSTRUCTIONS

*In rule 18, **room** is **room** for an inside boat to round* *or pass between an outside boat and a* **mark** *or* **obstruction**, *including* **room** *to tack or gybe when either is a normal part of the* manoeuvre.

18.1 When This Rule Applies
Rule 18 applies when boats are about to round or pass a *mark* they are required to leave on the same side, or an *obstruction* on the same side, until they have passed it. However, it does not apply

(a) at a starting *mark* surrounded by navigable water or at its anchor line from the time the boats are approaching them to *start* until they have passed them, or

(b) while the boats are on opposite *tacks*, either on a beat to windward or when the *proper course* for one of them, but not both, to round or pass the *mark* or *obstruction* is to tack.

18.2 Giving Room; Keeping Clear

(a) OVERLAPPED – BASIC RULE

When boats are *overlapped* the outside boat shall give the inside boat *room* to round or pass the *mark* or *obstruction*, and if the inside boat has right of way the outside boat shall also *keep clear*. Other parts of rule 18 contain exceptions to this rule.

(b) OVERLAPPED AT THE ZONE

If boats were *overlapped* before either of them reached the *two-length zone* and the *overlap* is broken after one of them has reached it, the boat that was on the outside shall continue to give the other boat *room*. If the outside boat becomes *clear astern* or *overlapped* inside the other boat, she is not entitled to *room* and shall *keep clear*.

(c) NOT OVERLAPPED AT THE ZONE

If a boat was *clear ahead* at the time she reached the *two-length zone*, the boat *clear astern* shall thereafter *keep clear*. If the boat *clear astern* becomes *overlapped* outside the other boat, she shall also give the inside boat *room*. If the boat *clear astern* becomes *overlapped* inside the other boat, she is not entitled to *room*. If the boat that was *clear ahead* passes head to wind, rule 18.2(c) no longer applies and remains inapplicable.

(d) CHANGING COURSE TO ROUND OR PASS

When after the starting signal rule 18 applies between two boats and the right-of-way boat is changing course to round or pass a *mark*, rule 16 does not apply between her and the other boat.

(e) OVERLAP RIGHTS

If there is reasonable doubt that a boat obtained or broke an *overlap* in time, it shall be presumed that she did not. If the outside boat is unable to give *room* when an *overlap* begins, rules 18.2(a) and 18.2(b) do not apply.

18.3 Tacking at a Mark
If two boats were approaching a *mark* on opposite *tacks* and one of them completes a tack in the *two-length zone* when the other is fetching the *mark*, rule 18.2 does not apply. The boat that tacked

(a) shall not cause the other boat to sail above close-hauled to avoid her or prevent the other boat from passing the *mark*, and

(b) shall give *room* if the other boat becomes *overlapped* inside her, in which case rule 15 does not apply.

18.4 Gybing
When an inside *overlapped* right-of-way boat must gybe at a *mark* or *obstruction* to sail her *proper course*, until she gybes she shall sail no farther from the *mark* or *obstruction* than needed to sail that course.

18.5 Passing a Continuing Obstruction
While boats are passing a continuing *obstruction*, rules 18.2(b) and 18.2(c) do not apply. A boat *clear astern* that obtains an inside *overlap* is entitled to *room* to pass between the other boat and the *obstruction* only if at the moment the *overlap* begins there is *room* to do so. If there is not, she is not entitled to *room* and shall *keep clear*.

19 ROOM TO TACK AT AN OBSTRUCTION
19.1 When approaching an *obstruction*, a boat sailing close-hauled or above may hail for *room* to tack and avoid another boat on the same *tack*. However, she shall not hail unless safety requires her to make a substantial course change to avoid the *obstruction*. Before tacking she shall give the hailed boat time to respond. The hailed boat shall respond by either

(a) tacking as soon as possible, in which case the hailing boat shall also tack as soon as possible, or

(b) immediately replying 'You tack', in which case the hailing boat shall tack as soon as possible and the hailed boat shall give *room*, and rules 10 and 13 do not apply.

19.2 Rule 19.1 does not apply at a starting *mark*

surrounded by navigable water or at its anchor line from the time boats are approaching them to *start* until they have passed them or at a *mark* that the hailed boat can fetch. When rule 19.1 applies, rule 18 does not.

SECTION D
OTHER RULES
When rule 20 or 21 applies between two boats, Section A rules do not.

20 STARTING ERRORS; PENALTY TURNS; MOVING ASTERN
20.1 A boat sailing towards the pre-start side of the starting line or its extensions after her starting signal to *start* or to comply with rule 30.1 shall *keep clear* of a boat not doing so until she is completely on the pre-start side.

20.2 A boat making a penalty turn shall *keep clear* of one that is not.

20.3 A boat moving astern by backing a sail shall *keep clear* of one that is not.

21 CAPSIZED, ANCHORED OR AGROUND; RESCUING
If possible, a boat shall avoid a boat that is capsized or has not regained control after capsizing, is anchored or aground, or is trying to help a person or vessel in danger. A boat is capsized when her masthead is in the water.

22 INTERFERING WITH ANOTHER BOAT
22.1 If reasonably possible, a boat not *racing* shall not interfere with a boat that is *racing*.

22.2 A boat shall not change course if her only purpose is to interfere with a boat making a penalty turn or one on another leg or lap of the course.

PART 3
CONDUCT OF A RACE

25 NOTICE OF RACE, SAILING INSTRUCTIONS AND SIGNALS
The notice of race and sailing instructions shall be made available to each boat before a race begins. The meanings of the visual and sound signals stated in Race Signals shall not be changed except under rule 86.1(b). The meanings of any other signals that may be used shall be stated in the sailing instructions.

26 STARTING RACES
Races shall be started by using the following signals. Times shall be taken from the visual signals; the absence of a sound signal shall be disregarded.

Signal	Flag and sound	Minutes before starting signal
Warning	Class flag; 1 sound	5*
Preparatory	P, I, Z, Z with I, or black flag; 1 sound	4
One-minute	Preparatory flag removed; 1 long sound	1
Starting	Class flag removed; 1 sound	0

*or as stated in the sailing instructions

The warning signal for each succeeding class shall be made with or after the starting signal of the preceding class.

27 OTHER RACE COMMITTEE ACTIONS BEFORE THE STARTING SIGNAL
27.1 No later than the warning signal, the race committee shall signal or otherwise designate the course to be sailed if the sailing instructions have not stated the course, and it may replace one course signal with another and signal that wearing personal buoyancy is required (display flag Y with one sound).

27.2 No later than the preparatory signal, the race committee may move a starting *mark* and may apply rule 30.

27.3 Before the starting signal, the race committee may for any reason *postpone* (display flag AP, AP over H, or AP over A, with two sounds) or *abandon* the race (display flag N over H, or N over A, with three sounds).

28 SAILING THE COURSE
28.1 A boat shall *start*, leave each *mark* on the required side in the correct order, and *finish*, so that a string representing her wake after *starting* and until *finishing* would when drawn taut pass each *mark* on the required side and touch each rounding *mark*. She may correct any errors to comply with this rule. After *finishing* she need not cross the finishing line completely.

28.2 A boat may leave on either side a *mark* that does not begin, bound or end the leg she is on. However, she shall leave a starting *mark* on the required side when she is approaching the starting line from its pre-start side to *start*.

29 RECALLS
29.1 Individual Recall
When at a boat's starting signal any part of her hull, crew or equipment is on the course side of

the starting line or she must comply with rule 30.1, the race committee shall promptly display flag X with one sound. The flag shall be displayed until all such boats are completely on the pre-start side of the starting line or its extensions and have complied with rule 30.1 if it applies, but not later than four minutes after the starting signal or one minute before any later starting signal, whichever is earlier.

29.2 General Recall
When at the starting signal the race committee is unable to identify boats that are on the course side of the starting line or to which rule 30 applies, or there has been an error in the starting procedure, the race committee may signal a general recall (display the First Substitute with two sounds). The warning signal for a new start for the recalled class shall be made one minute after the First Substitute is removed (one sound), and the starts for any succeeding classes shall follow the new start.

30 STARTING PENALTIES
30.1 Round-an-End Rule
If flag I has been displayed, and any part of a boat's hull, crew or equipment is on the course side of the starting line or its extensions during the minute before her starting signal, she shall thereafter sail from the course side across an extension to the pre-start side before *starting*.

30.2 20% Penalty Rule
If flag Z has been displayed, no part of a boat's hull, crew or equipment shall be in the triangle formed by the ends of the starting line and the first *mark* during the minute before her starting signal. If a boat breaks this rule and is identified, she shall receive, without a hearing, a 20% scoring penalty calculated as stated in rule 44.3(c). She shall be penalized even if the race is restarted, resailed or rescheduled, but not if it is *postponed* or *abandoned* before the starting signal.

30.3 Black Flag Rule
If a black flag has been displayed, no part of a boat's hull, crew or equipment shall be in the triangle formed by the ends of the starting line and the first *mark* during the minute before her starting signal. If a boat breaks this rule and is identified, she shall be disqualified without a hearing, even if the race is restarted, resailed or rescheduled, but not if it is *postponed* or *abandoned* before the starting signal. If a general recall is signalled or the race is *abandoned* after the starting signal, the race committee shall display her sail number before the next warning signal for that race, and if the race is restarted or resailed she shall not sail in it. If she does so, her disqualification shall not be excluded in calculating her series score.If this rule applies rule 29.1 does not.

31 TOUCHING A MARK
31.1 While *racing*, a boat shall not touch a starting *mark* before *starting*, a *mark* that begins, bounds or ends the leg of the course on which she is sailing, or a finishing *mark* after *finishing*.

31.2 A boat that has broken rule 31.1 may, after getting well clear of other boats as soon as possible, take a penalty by promptly making one turn including one tack and one gybe. When a boat takes the penalty after touching a finishing *mark*, she shall sail completely to the course side of the line before *finishing*. However, if a boat has gained a significant advantage in the race or series by touching the *mark* her penalty shall be to retire.

32 SHORTENING OR ABANDONING AFTER THE START
32.1 After the starting signal, the race committee may shorten the course (display flag S with two sounds) or *abandon* the race (display flag N, N over H, or N over A, with three sounds), as appropriate,

(a) because of an error in the starting procedure,

(b) because of foul weather,

(c) because of insufficient wind making it unlikely that any boat will *finish* within the time limit,

(d) because a *mark* is missing or out of position, or

(e) for any other reason directly affecting the safety or fairness of the competition,
or may shorten the course so that other scheduled races can be sailed. However, after one boat has sailed the course and *finished* within the time limit, if any, the race committee shall not *abandon* the race without considering the consequences for all boats in the race or series.

32.2 If the race committee signals a shortened course (displays flag S with two sounds), the finishing line shall be,

(a) at a rounding *mark*, between the *mark* and a staff displaying flag S;

(b) at a line boats are required to cross at the end of each lap, that line;

(c) at a gate, between the gate *marks*.

33 CHANGING THE NEXT LEG OF THE COURSE
The race committee may change a leg of the course that begins at a rounding *mark* by changing the position of the next *mark* (or the finishing line) and signalling all boats before they begin the leg.

The next *mark* need not be in position at that time.

(a) If the direction of the leg will be changed, the signal shall be the display of flag C with repetitive sounds and either

(1) the new compass bearing or
(2) a green triangular flag or board for a change to starboard or a red rectangular flag or board for a change to port.

(b) If the length of the leg will be changed, the signal shall be the display of flag C with repetitive sounds and a '–' if the leg will be shortened or a '+' if the leg will be lengthened.

(c) Subsequent legs may be changed without further signalling to maintain the course shape.

34 MARK MISSING
If a *mark* is missing or out of position, the race committee shall, if possible,

(a) replace it in its correct position or substitute a new one of similar appearance, or

(b) substitute an object displaying flag M and make repetitive sound signals.

35 TIME LIMIT AND SCORES
If one boat sails the course as required by rule 28.1 and *finishes* within the time limit, if any, all boats that *finish* shall be scored according to their finishing places unless the race is *abandoned*. If no boat *finishes* within the time limit, the race committee shall *abandon* the race.

36 RACES RESTARTED OR RESAILED
If a race is restarted or resailed, a breach of a *rule*, other than rule 30.3, in the original race shall not prohibit a boat from competing or, except under rule 30.2, 30.3 or 69, cause her to be penalized.

PART 4
OTHER REQUIREMENTS WHEN RACING

*Part 4 rules apply only to boats **racing**.*

40 PERSONAL BUOYANCY; HARNESSES
40.1 When flag Y is displayed with one sound before or with the warning signal, competitors shall wear life-jackets or other adequate personal buoyancy. Wet suits and dry suits are not adequate personal buoyancy.

40.2 A trapeze or hiking harness shall have a device that can quickly release the competitor from the boat at any time while in use.

Note: This rule takes effect on 1 January 2006.

41 OUTSIDE HELP
A boat shall not receive help from any outside source, except

(a) help as provided for in rule 1;

(b) help for an ill or injured crew member;

(c) after a collision, help from the crew of the other boat to get clear;

(d) help in the form of information freely available to all boats;

(e) unsolicited information from a disinterested source, which may be another boat in the same race.

42 PROPULSION
42.1 Basic Rule
Except when permitted in rule 42.3 or 45, a boat shall compete by using only the wind and water to increase, maintain or decrease her speed. Her crew may adjust the trim of sails and hull, and perform other acts of seamanship, but shall not otherwise move their bodies to propel the boat.

42.2 Prohibited Actions
Without limiting the application of rule 42.1, these actions are prohibited:

(a) pumping: repeated fanning of any sail either by pulling in and releasing the sail or by vertical or athwartships body movement;

(b) rocking: repeated rolling of the boat, induced by
(1) body movement,
(2) repeated adjustment of the sails or centreboard, or
(3) steering;

(c) ooching: sudden forward body movement, stopped abruptly;

(d) sculling: repeated movement of the helm that is either forceful or that propels the boat forward or prevents her from moving astern;

(e) repeated tacks or gybes unrelated to changes in the wind or to tactical considerations.

42.3 Exceptions
(a) A boat may be rolled to facilitate steering.

(b) A boat's crew may move their bodies to exaggerate the rolling that facilitates steering the boat through a tack or a gybe, provided that, just after the tack or gybe is completed, the boat's speed is not greater than it would have been in the absence of the tack or gybe.

(c) Except on a beat to windward, when surfing (rapidly accelerating down the leeward side of a wave) or planing is possible, the boat's crew may pull the sheet and the guy controlling any sail in order to initiate surfing or planing, but only once for each wave or gust of wind.

(d) When a boat is above a close-hauled course and either stationary or moving slowly, she may scull to turn to a close-hauled course.

(e) A boat may reduce speed by repeatedly moving her helm.

(f) Any means of propulsion may be used to help a person or another vessel in danger.

(g) To get clear after grounding or colliding with another boat or object, a boat may use force applied by the crew of either boat and any equipment other than a propulsion engine. *Note: Interpretations of rule 42 are available at the ISAF website (www.sailing.org) or by mail upon request.*

43 COMPETITOR CLOTHING AND EQUIPMENT

43.1 (a) Competitors shall not wear or carry clothing or equipment for the purpose of increasing their weight.

(b) Furthermore, a competitor's clothing and equipment shall not weigh more than 8 kilograms, excluding a hiking or trapeze harness and clothing (including footwear) worn only below the knee. Class rules or sailing instructions may specify a lower weight or a higher weight up to 10 kilograms. Class rules may include footwear and other clothing worn below the knee within that weight. A hiking or trapeze harness shall have positive buoyancy and shall not weigh more than 2 kilograms, except that class rules may specify a higher weight up to 4 kilograms. Weights shall be determined as required by Appendix H.

(c) When a measurer in charge of weighing clothing and equipment believes a competitor may have broken rule 43.1(a) or 43.1(b) he shall report the matter in writing to the race committee, which shall protest the boat of the competitor.

43.2 Rule 43.1(b) does not apply to boats required to be equipped with lifelines.

44 PENALTIES FOR BREAKING RULES OF PART 2

44.1 Taking a Penalty

A boat that may have broken a rule of Part 2 while *racing* may take a penalty at the time of the incident. Her penalty shall be a Two-Turns Penalty unless the sailing instructions specify the use of the Scoring Penalty or some other penalty. However, if she caused injury or serious damage or gained a significant advantage in the race or series by her breach her penalty shall be to retire.

44.2 Two-Turns Penalty

After getting well clear of other boats as soon after the incident as possible, a boat takes a Two-Turns Penalty by promptly making two turns in the same direction, including two tacks and two gybes. When a boat takes the penalty at or near the finishing line, she shall sail completely to the course side of the line before *finishing*.

44.3 Scoring Penalty

(a) A boat takes a Scoring Penalty by displaying a yellow flag at the first reasonable opportunity after the incident, keeping it displayed until *finishing*, and calling the race committee's attention to it at the finishing line. At that time she shall also inform the race committee of the identity of the other boat involved in the incident. If this is impracticable, she shall do so at the first reasonable opportunity within the time limit for *protests*.

(b) If a boat displays a yellow flag, she shall also comply with the other parts of rule 44.3(a).

(c) The boat's penalty score shall be the score for the place worse than her actual finishing place by the number of places stated in the sailing instructions, except that she shall not be scored worse than Did Not Finish. When the sailing instructions do not state the number of places, the number shall be the whole number (rounding 0.5 upward) nearest to 20% of the number of boats entered. The scores of other boats shall not be changed; therefore, two boats may receive the same score.

44.4 Limits on Penalties

(a) When a boat intends to take a penalty as provided in rule 44.1 and in the same incident has touched a *mark*, she need not take the penalty provided in rule 31.2.

(b) A boat that takes a penalty shall not be penalized further with respect to the same incident unless she failed to retire when rule 44.1 required her to do so.

45 HAULING OUT; MAKING FAST; ANCHORING

A boat shall be afloat and off moorings at her preparatory signal. Thereafter, she shall not be hauled out or made fast except to bail out, reef sails or make repairs. She may anchor or the crew may stand on the bottom. She shall recover the anchor before continuing in the race unless she is unable to do so.

46 PERSON IN CHARGE

A boat shall have on board a person in charge designated by the member or organization that entered the boat. See rule 75.

47 LIMITATIONS ON EQUIPMENT AND CREW

47.1 A boat shall use only the equipment on board at her preparatory signal.

47.2 No person on board shall intentionally leave, except when ill or injured, or to help a person or vessel in danger, or to swim. A person leaving the boat by accident or to swim shall be back on board before the boat continues in the race.

48 FOG SIGNALS AND LIGHTS

When safety requires, a boat shall sound fog signals and show lights as required by the *International Regulations for Preventing Collisions at Sea* or applicable government rules.

49 CREW POSITION

49.1 Competitors shall use no device designed to position their bodies outboard, other than hiking straps and stiffeners worn under the thighs.

49.2 When lifelines are required by the class rules or the sailing instructions they shall be taut, and competitors shall not position any part of their torsos outside them, except briefly to perform a necessary task. On boats equipped with upper and lower lifelines of wire, a competitor sitting on the deck facing outboard with his waist inside the lower lifeline may have the upper part of his body outside the upper lifeline.

50 SETTING AND SHEETING SAILS
50.1 Changing Sails

When headsails or spinnakers are being changed, a replacing sail may be fully set and trimmed before the replaced sail is lowered. However, only one mainsail and, except when changing, only one spinnaker shall be carried set at a time.

50.2 Spinnaker Poles; Whisker Poles

Only one spinnaker pole or whisker pole shall be used at a time except when gybing. When in use, it shall be attached to the foremost mast.

50.3 Use of Outriggers

(a) No sail shall be sheeted over or through an outrigger, except as permitted in rule 50.3(b) or 50.3(c). An outrigger is any fitting or other device so placed that it could exert outward pressure on a sheet or sail at a point from which, with the boat upright, a vertical line would fall outside the hull or deck planking. For the purpose of this rule, bulwarks, rails and rubbing strakes are not part of the hull or deck planking and the following are not outriggers: a bowsprit used to secure the tack of a working sail, a bumkin used to sheet the boom of a working sail, or a boom of a boomed headsail that requires no adjustment when tacking.

(b) Any sail may be sheeted to or led above a boom that is regularly used for a working sail and is permanently attached to the mast from which the head of the working sail is set.

(c) A headsail may be sheeted or attached at its clew to a spinnaker pole or whisker pole, provided that a spinnaker is not set.

50.4 Headsails

The difference between a headsail and a spinnaker is that the mid-girth of a headsail, measured from the mid-points of its luff and leech, does not exceed 50% of the length of its foot, and no other intermediate girth exceeds a percentage similarly proportional to its distance from the head of the sail. A sail tacked down behind the foremost mast is not a headsail.

51 MOVABLE BALLAST

All movable ballast shall be properly stowed, and water, dead weight or ballast shall not be moved for the purpose of changing trim or stability. Floorboards, bulkheads, doors, stairs and water tanks shall be left in place and all cabin fixtures kept on board.

52 MANUAL POWER

A boat's standing rigging, running rigging, spars and movable hull appendages shall be adjusted and operated only by manual power.

53 SKIN FRICTION

A boat shall not eject or release a substance, such as a polymer, or have specially textured surfaces that could improve the character of the flow of water inside the boundary layer.

54 FORESTAYS AND HEADSAIL TACKS

Forestays and headsail tacks, except those of spinnaker staysails when the boat is not close-hauled, shall be attached approximately on a boat's centreline.

PART 5
PROTESTS, REDRESS, HEARINGS, MISCONDUCT AND APPEALS

SECTION A
PROTESTS; REDRESS; RULE 69 ACTION

60 RIGHT TO PROTEST; RIGHT TO REQUEST REDRESS OR RULE 69 ACTION

60.1 A boat may

(a) protest another boat, but not for an alleged breach of a rule of Part 2 unless she was involved in or saw the incident; or

(b) request redress.

60.2 A race committee may

(a) protest a boat, but not as a result of a report from an *interested party* or information in an invalid *protest* or in a request for redress;

(b) request redress for a boat; or

(c) report to the protest committee requesting action under rule 69.1(a).

60.3 A protest committee may

(a) protest a boat, but not as a result of a report from an *interested party* or information in an invalid *protest* or in a request for redress. However, it may protest a boat
(1) if it learns of an incident involving her that may have resulted in injury or serious damage, or
(2) if during the hearing of a valid *protest* it learns that the boat, although not a *party* to the hearing, was involved in the incident and may have broken a *rule*;

(b) call a hearing to consider redress; or

(c) act under rule 69.1(a).

61 PROTEST REQUIREMENTS
61.1 Informing the Protestee
(a) A boat intending to protest shall inform the other boat at the first reasonable opportunity. When her *protest* concerns an incident in the racing area that she is involved in or sees, she shall hail 'Protest' and conspicuously display a red flag at the first reasonable opportunity for each. She shall display the flag until she is no longer *racing*. However,
(1) if the other boat is beyond hailing distance, the protesting boat need not hail but she shall inform the other boat at the first reasonable opportunity;
(2) if the hull length of the protesting boat is less than 6 metres, she need not display a red flag;
(3) if the incident results in damage or injury that is obvious to the boats involved and one of them intends to protest, the requirements of this rule do not apply to her, but she shall attempt to inform the other boat within the time limit of rule 61.3.

(b) A race committee or protest committee intending to protest a boat shall inform her as soon as reasonably possible. However, if the *protest* arises from an incident the committee observes in the racing area, it shall inform the boat after the race within the time limit of rule 61.3.

(c) If the protest committee decides to protest a boat under rule 60.3(a)(2), it shall inform her as soon as reasonably possible, close the current hearing, proceed as required by rules 61.2 and 63, and hear the original and the new *protests* together.

61.2 Protest Contents
A *protest* shall be in writing and identify

(a) the protestor and protestee;

(b) the incident, including where and when it occurred;

(c) any *rule* the protestor believes was broken; and

(d) the name of the protestor's representative.
However, if requirement (b) is met, requirement (a) may be met at any time before the hearing, and requirements (c) and (d) may be met before or during the hearing.

61.3 Protest Time Limit
A *protest* by a boat, or by the race committee or protest committee about an incident the committee observes in the racing area, shall be delivered to the race office no later than the time limit stated in the sailing instructions. If none is stated, the time limit is two hours after the last boat in the race *finishes*. Other race committee or protest committee *protests* shall be delivered to the race office within two hours after the committee receives the relevant information. The protest committee shall extend the time if there is good reason to do so.

62 REDRESS
62.1 A request for redress or a protest committee's decision to consider redress shall be based on a claim or possibility that a boat's score in a race or series has, through no fault of her own, been made significantly worse by

(a) an improper action or omission of the race committee, protest committee or organizing authority;

(b) injury or physical damage because of the action of a boat that was breaking a rule of Part 2 or of a vessel not *racing* that was required to keep clear;

(c) giving help (except to herself or her crew) in compliance with rule 1.1; or

(d) a boat against which a penalty has been imposed under rule 2 or disciplinary action has been taken under rule 69.1(b).

62.2 The request shall be made in writing within the time limit of rule 61.3 or within two hours of the relevant incident, whichever is later. The protest committee shall extend the time if there is good reason to do so. No red flag is required.

SECTION B
HEARINGS AND DECISIONS

63 HEARINGS
63.1 Requirement for a Hearing
A boat or competitor shall not be penalized without a protest hearing, except as provided in rules 30.2, 30.3, 67, 69, A5 and P2. A decision on redress shall not be made without a hearing. The protest committee shall hear all *protests* and requests for redress that have been delivered to the race office unless it allows a *protest* or request to be withdrawn.

63.2 Time and Place of the Hearing; Time for Parties to Prepare
All *parties* to the hearing shall be notified of the time and place of the hearing, the *protest* or redress information shall be made available to them, and they shall be allowed reasonable time to prepare for the hearing.

63.3 Right to Be Present
(a) The *parties* to the hearing, or a representative of each, have the right to be present throughout the hearing of all the evidence. When a *protest* claims a breach of a rule of Part 2, 3 or 4, the representatives of boats shall have been on board at the time of the incident, unless there is good reason for the protest committee to rule otherwise. Any witness, other than a member of the protest committee, shall be excluded except when giving evidence.

(b) If a *party* to the hearing does not come to the hearing, the protest committee may nevertheless decide the *protest* or request for redress. If the *party* was unavoidably absent, the committee may reopen the hearing.

63.4 Interested Party

A member of a protest committee who is an *interested party* shall not take any further part in the hearing but may appear as a witness. A *party* to the hearing who believes a member of the protest committee is an *interested party* shall object as soon as possible.

63.5 Validity of the Protest or Request for Redress

At the beginning of the hearing the protest committee shall decide whether all requirements for the *protest* or request for redress have been met, after first taking any evidence it considers necessary. If all requirements have been met, the *protest* or request is valid and the hearing shall be continued. If not, it shall be closed. If the *protest* has been made under rule 60.3(a)(1), the protest committee shall also determine whether or not injury or serious damage resulted from the incident in question. If not, the hearing shall be closed.

63.6 Taking Evidence and Finding Facts

The protest committee shall take the evidence of the *parties* to the hearing and of their witnesses and other evidence it considers necessary. A member of the protest committee who saw the incident may give evidence. A *party* to the hearing may question any person who gives evidence. The committee shall then find the facts and base its decision on them.

63.7 Conflict between Rules

If there is a conflict between a *rule* in the notice of race and one in the sailing instructions that must be resolved before the protest committee can decide a *protest* or request for redress, the committee shall apply the *rule* that it believes will provide the fairest result for all boats affected.

63.8 Protests between Boats in Different Races

A *protest* between boats sailing in different races conducted by different organizing authorities shall be heard by a protest committee acceptable to those authorities.

64 DECISIONS

64.1 Penalties and Exoneration

(a) When the protest committee decides that a boat that is a *party* to a protest hearing has broken a *rule*, it shall disqualify her unless some other penalty applies. A penalty shall be imposed whether or not the applicable *rule* was mentioned in the *protest*.

(b) When as a consequence of breaking a *rule* a boat has compelled another boat to break a *rule*, rule 64.1(a) does not apply to the other boat and she shall be exonerated.

(c) If a boat has broken a *rule* when not *racing*, her penalty shall apply to the race sailed nearest in time to that of the incident.

64.2 Decisions on Redress

When the protest committee decides that a boat is entitled to redress under rule 62, it shall make as fair an arrangement as possible for all boats affected, whether or not they asked for redress. This may be to adjust the scoring (see rule A10 for some examples) or finishing times of boats, to *abandon* the race, to let the results stand or to make some other arrangement. When in doubt about the facts or probable results of any arrangement for the race or series, especially before *abandoning* the race, the protest committee shall take evidence from appropriate sources.

64.3 Decisions on Measurement Protests

(a) When the protest committee finds that deviations in excess of tolerances specified in the class rules were caused by damage or normal wear and do not improve the performance of the boat, it shall not penalize her. However, the boat shall

not *race* again until the deviations have been corrected, except when the protest committee decides there is or has been no reasonable opportunity to do so.

(b) When the protest committee is in doubt about the meaning of a measurement rule, it shall refer its questions, together with the relevant facts, to an authority responsible for interpreting the rule. In making its decision, the committee shall be bound by the reply of the authority.

(c) When a boat disqualified under a measurement rule states in writing that she intends to appeal, she may compete in subsequent races without changes to the boat, but shall be disqualified if she fails to appeal or the appeal is decided against her.

(d) Measurement costs arising from a *protest* involving a measurement rule shall be paid by the unsuccessful *party* unless the protest committee decides otherwise.

65 INFORMING THE PARTIES AND OTHERS

65.1 After making its decision, the protest committee shall promptly inform the *parties* to the hearing of the facts found, the applicable *rules*, the decision, the reasons for it, and any penalties imposed or redress given.

65.2 A *party* to the hearing is entitled to receive the above information in writing, provided she asks for it in writing from the protest committee within seven days of being informed of the decision. The committee shall then promptly provide the information, including, when relevant, a diagram of the incident prepared or endorsed by the committee.

65.3 When the protest committee penalizes a boat under a measurement rule, it shall send the above information to the relevant measurement authorities.

66 REOPENING A HEARING

The protest committee may reopen a hearing when it decides that it may have made a significant error, or when significant new evidence becomes available within a reasonable time. It shall reopen a hearing when required by the national authority under rule F5. A *party* to the hearing may ask for a reopening no later than 24 hours after being informed of the decision. When a hearing is reopened, a majority of the members of the protest committee shall, if possible, be members of the original protest committee.

67 RULE 42 AND HEARING REQUIREMENT

When so stated in the sailing instructions, the protest committee may penalize without a hearing a boat that has broken rule 42, provided that a member of the committee or its designated observer has seen the incident, and a disqualification under this rule shall not be excluded from the boat's series score. A boat so penalized shall be informed by notification in the race results.

68 DAMAGES

The question of damages arising from a breach of any *rule* shall be governed by the prescriptions, if any, of the national authority.

SECTION C
GROSS MISCONDUCT

69 ALLEGATIONS OF GROSS MISCONDUCT

69.1 Action by a Protest Committee

(a) When a protest committee, from its own observation or a report received from any source, believes that a competitor may have committed a gross breach of a *rule*, good manners or sportsmanship, or may have brought the sport into disrepute, it may call a hearing. The protest committee shall promptly inform the competitor in writing of the alleged misconduct and of the time and place of the hearing.

(b) A protest committee of at least three members shall

conduct the hearing, following rules 63.2, 63.3, 63.4 and 63.6. If it decides that the competitor committed the alleged misconduct it shall either

(1) warn the competitor or

(2) impose a penalty by excluding the competitor and, when appropriate, disqualifying a boat, from a race or the remaining races or all races of the series, or by taking other action within its jurisdiction. A disqualification under this rule shall not be excluded from the boat's series score.

(c) The protest committee shall promptly report a penalty, but not a warning, to the national authorities of the venue, of the competitor and of the boat owner.

(d) If there is good reason for the competitor not to attend the hearing, the protest committee shall postpone it. However, if the competitor has left the event and as a result cannot reasonably be expected to attend a hearing, the protest committee shall not conduct one. Instead, it shall collect all available information and, if the allegation seems justified, make a report to the relevant national authorities.

(e) When the protest committee has left the event and a report alleging misconduct is received, the race committee or organizing authority may appoint a new protest committee to proceed under this rule.

69.2 Action by a National Authority

(a) When a national authority receives a report required by rule 69.1(c) or 69.1(d), a report alleging a gross breach of a *rule*, good manners or sportsmanship, or a report alleging conduct that has brought the sport into disrepute, it may conduct an investigation and, when appropriate, shall conduct a hearing. It may then take any disciplinary action within its jurisdiction it considers appropriate against the competitor or boat, or other person involved, including suspending eligibility, permanently or for a specified period of time, to compete in any event held within its jurisdiction, and suspending ISAF eligibility under ISAF Regulation 19.

(b) The national authority of a competitor shall also suspend the ISAF eligibility of the competitor as required in ISAF Regulation 19.

(c) The national authority shall promptly report a suspension of eligibility under rule 69.2(a) to the ISAF, and to the national authorities of the person or the owner of the boat suspended if they are not members of the suspending national authority.

69.3 Action by the ISAF

Upon receipt of a report required by rule 69.2(c) or ISAF Regulation 19, the ISAF shall inform all national authorities, which may also suspend eligibility for events held within their jurisdiction. The ISAF Executive Committee shall suspend the competitor's ISAF eligibility as required in ISAF Regulation 19 if the competitor's national authority does not do so.

SECTION D
APPEALS

70 APPEALS; CONFIRMATION OR CORRECTION OF DECISIONS; RULE INTERPRETATIONS

70.1 Provided that the right of appeal has not been denied under rule 70.4, a *party* to a hearing may appeal a protest committee's decision or its procedures, but not the facts found, to the national authority of the venue.

70.2 A protest committee may request confirmation or correction of its decision.

70.3 A club or other organization affiliated to a national authority may request an interpretation of the *rules*, provided that no *protest* or request for redress that may be appealed is involved. The interpretation shall not be used for changing a previous protest committee decision.

70.4 There shall be no appeal from the decisions of an international jury constituted in compliance with Appendix N. Furthermore, if the notice of race and the sailing instructions so state, the right of appeal may be denied provided that

(a) it is essential to determine promptly the result of a race that will qualify a boat to compete in a later stage of an event or a subsequent event (a national authority may prescribe that its approval is required for such a procedure);

(b) a national authority so approves for a particular event open only to entrants under its own jurisdiction; or

(c) a national authority after consultation with the ISAF so approves for a particular event, provided the protest committee is constituted as required by Appendix N, except that only two members of the protest committee need be International Judges.

70.5 Appeals and requests shall conform to Appendix F.

71 APPEAL DECISIONS

71.1 No *interested party* or member of the protest committee shall take any part in the discussion or decision on an appeal or a request for confirmation or correction.

71.2 The national authority may uphold, change or reverse the protest committee's decision; declare the *protest* or request for redress invalid; or return the *protest* or request for the hearing to be reopened, or for a new hearing and decision by the same or a different protest committee.

71.3 When from the facts found by the protest committee the national authority decides that a boat that was a *party* to a protest hearing broke a *rule*, it shall penalize her, whether or not that boat or that *rule* was mentioned in the protest committee's decision.

71.4 The decision of the national authority shall be final. The national authority shall send its decision in writing to all *parties* to the hearing and the protest committee, who shall be bound by the decision.

PART 6
ENTRY AND QUALIFICATION

75 ENTERING A RACE

75.1 To enter a race, a boat shall comply with the requirements of the organizing authority of the race. She shall be entered by

(a) a member of a club or other organization affiliated to an ISAF member national authority,

(b) such a club or organization, or

(c) a member of an ISAF member national authority.

75.2 Competitors shall comply with ISAF Regulation 19, Eligibility Code.

76 EXCLUSION OF BOATS OR COMPETITORS

76.1 The organizing authority or the race committee may reject or cancel the entry of a boat or exclude a competitor, subject to rule 76.2, provided it does so before the start of the first race and states the reason for doing so. However, the organizing authority or the race committee shall not reject or cancel the entry of a boat or exclude a competitor because of advertising, provided the boat or competitor complies with ISAF Regulation 20, Advertising Code.

76.2 At world and continental championships no entry within stated quotas shall be rejected or cancelled without first obtaining the approval of the relevant international class association (or the Offshore Racing Council) or the ISAF.

77 IDENTIFICATION ON SAILS

A boat shall comply with the requirements of Appendix G governing class insignia, national letters and numbers on sails.

78 COMPLIANCE WITH CLASS RULES; CERTIFICATES

78.1 A boat's owner and any other person in charge shall ensure that the boat is maintained to comply with her class rules and that her measurement or rating certificate, if any, remains valid.

78.2 When a *rule* requires a certificate to be produced before a boat *races*, and it is not produced, the boat may *race* provided that the race committee receives a statement signed by the person in charge that a valid certificate exists and that it will be given to the race committee before the end of the event. If the certificate is not received in time, the boat shall be disqualified from all races of the event.

78.3 When a measurer for an event decides that a boat or personal equipment does not comply with the class rules, he shall report the matter in writing to the race committee, which shall protest the boat.

79 ADVERTISING

A boat and her crew shall comply with ISAF Regulation 20, Advertising Code.

80 RESCHEDULED RACES

When a race has been rescheduled, rule 36 applies and all boats entered in the original race shall be notified and, unless disqualified under rule 30.3, be entitled to sail the rescheduled race. New entries that meet the entry requirements of the original race may be accepted at the discretion of the race committee.

PART 7
RACE ORGANIZATION

85 GOVERNING RULES

The organizing authority, race committee and protest committee shall be governed by the *rules* in the conduct and judging of races.

86 CHANGES TO THE RACING RULES

86.1 A racing rule shall not be changed unless permitted in the rule itself or as follows:

(a) Prescriptions of a national authority may change a racing rule, but not the Definitions; a rule in the Introduction; Sportsmanship and the Rules; Part 1, 2 or 7; rule 42, 43.1, 43.2, 69, 70, 71, 75, 76.2 or 79; a rule of an appendix that changes one of these rules; Appendix H or N; or ISAF Regulation 19, 20 or 21.

(b) Sailing instructions may change a racing rule by referring specifically to it and stating the change, but not rule 76.1, Appendix F, or a rule listed in rule 86.1(a).

(c) Class rules may change only racing rules 42, 49, 50, 51, 52, 53 and 54.

86.2 In exception to rule 86.1, the ISAF may in limited circumstances (see ISAF Regulation 31.1.3) authorize changes to the racing rules for a specific international event. The authorization shall be stated in a letter of approval to the event organizing authority and in the notice of race and sailing instructions, and the letter shall be posted on the event's official notice board.

86.3 If a national authority so prescribes, these restrictions do not apply if rules are changed to develop or test proposed rules. The national authority may prescribe that its approval is required for such changes.

87 CHANGES TO NATIONAL AUTHORITY PRESCRIPTIONS

A national authority may restrict changes to its prescriptions with a prescription to this rule. If it does so, that prescription shall not be changed or deleted by sailing instructions.

88 ORGANIZING AUTHORITY; NOTICE OF RACE; APPOINTMENT OF RACE OFFICIALS

88.1 Organizing Authority

Races shall be organized by an organizing authority, which shall be

(a) the ISAF;

(b) a member national authority of the ISAF;

(c) a club or other organization affiliated to a national authority;

(d) a class association, either with the approval of a national authority or in conjunction with an affiliated club;

(e) an unaffiliated body in conjunction with an affiliated club where the body is owned and controlled by the club. The national authority of the club may prescribe that its approval is required for such an event; or

(f) if approved by the ISAF and the national authority of the club, an unaffiliated body in conjunction with an affiliated club where the body is not owned and controlled by the club.

88.2 Notice of Race; Appointment of Race Officials

(a) The organizing authority shall publish a notice of race that conforms to rule J1. The notice of race may be changed provided adequate notice is given.

(b) The organizing authority shall appoint a race committee and, when appropriate, appoint a protest committee and umpires. However, the race committee, an international jury and umpires may be appointed by the ISAF as provided in the ISAF regulations.

89 RACE COMMITTEE; SAILING INSTRUCTIONS; SCORING

89.1 Race Committee

The race committee shall conduct races as directed by the organizing authority and as required by the *rules*.

89.2 Sailing Instructions

(a) The race committee shall publish written sailing instructions that conform to rule J2.

(b) The sailing instructions for an international event shall include, in English, the applicable prescriptions of the national authority.

(c) Changes to the sailing instructions shall be in writing and posted within the required time on the official notice board or, on the water, communicated to each boat before her warning signal. Oral changes may be given only on the water, and only if the procedure is stated in the sailing instructions.

89.3 Scoring

(a) The race committee shall score a race or series as provided in Appendix A using the Low Point System, unless the sailing instructions specify the Bonus Point System or some other system. A race shall be scored if it is not *abandoned* and if one boat sails the course in compliance with rule 28.1 and *finishes* within the time limit, if any, even if she retires after *finishing* or is disqualified.

(b) When a scoring system provides for excluding one or more race scores from a boat's series score, the score for disqualification under rule 2; rule 30.3's next-to-last sentence; rule 42 if rule 67, P2.2 or P2.3 applies; or rule 69.1(b)(2) shall not be excluded. The next-worse score shall be excluded instead.

90 PROTEST COMMITTEE

A protest committee shall be

(a) a committee appointed by the organizing authority or race committee, or

(b) an international jury appointed by the organizing authority or as prescribed in the ISAF regulations and meeting the requirements of Appendix N. A national authority may prescribe that its approval is required for the appointment of international juries for races within its jurisdiction, except ISAF events or when international juries are appointed by the ISAF under rule 88.2(b).

APPENDIX A
SCORING

See rule 89.3.

A1 NUMBER OF RACES

The number of races scheduled and the number required to be completed to constitute a series shall be stated in the sailing instructions.

A2 SERIES SCORES

Each boat's series score shall be the total of her race scores excluding her worst score. (The sailing instructions may make a different arrangement by providing, for example, that no score will be excluded, that two or more scores will be excluded, or that a specified number of scores will be excluded if a specified number of races are completed. A race is completed if scored; see rule 89.3(a).) If a boat has two or more equal worst scores, the score(s) for the race(s) sailed earliest in the series shall be excluded. The boat with the lowest series score wins and others shall be ranked accordingly.

A3 STARTING TIMES AND FINISHING PLACES

The time of a boat's starting signal shall be her starting time, and the order in which boats *finish* a race shall determine their finishing places. However, when a handicap or rating system is used a boat's corrected time shall determine her finishing place.

A4 LOW POINT AND BONUS POINT SYSTEMS

Most series are scored using either the Low Point System or the Bonus Point System. The Low Point System uses a boat's finishing place as her race score. The Bonus Point System benefits the first six finishers because of the greater difficulty in advancing from fourth place to third, for example, than from fourteenth place to thirteenth. The Low Point System will apply unless the sailing instructions specify another system; see rule 89.3(a). If the Bonus Point System is chosen it can be made to apply by stating in the sailing instructions that 'The Bonus Point System of Appendix A will apply.'

A4.1 Each boat *starting* and *finishing* and not thereafter retiring, being penalized or given redress shall be scored points as follows:

Finishing place	Low Point System	Bonus Point System
First	1	0
Second	2	3
Third	3	5.7
Fourth	4	8
Fifth	5	10
Sixth	6	11.7
Seventh	7	13
Each place thereafter	Add 1 point	Add 1 point

A4.2 A boat that did not *start*, did not *finish*, retired after finishing or was disqualified shall be scored points for the

finishing place one more than the number of boats entered in the series. A boat penalized under rule 30.2 or 44.3 shall be scored points as provided in rule 44.3(c).

A5 SCORES DETERMINED BY THE RACE COMMITTEE

A boat that did not *start*, comply with rule 30.2 or 30.3, or *finish*, or that takes a penalty under rule 44.3 or retires after *finishing*, shall be scored accordingly by the race committee without a hearing. Only the protest committee may take other scoring actions that worsen a boat's score.

A6 CHANGES IN PLACES AND SCORES OF OTHER BOATS

A6.1 If a boat is disqualified from a race or retires after *finishing*, each boat with a worse finishing place shall be moved up one place.

A6.2 If the protest committee decides to give redress by adjusting a boat's score, the scores of other boats shall not be changed unless the protest committee decides otherwise.

A7 RACE TIES

If boats are tied at the finishing line or if a handicap or rating system is used and boats have equal corrected times, the points for the place for which the boats have tied and for the place(s) immediately below shall be added together and divided equally. Boats tied for a race prize shall share it or be given equal prizes.

A8 SERIES TIES

A8.1 If there is a series score tie between two or more boats, each boat's race scores shall be listed in order of best to worst, and at the first point(s) where there is a difference the tie shall be broken in favour of the boat(s) with the best score(s). No excluded scores shall be used.

A8.2 If a tie remains between two or more boats, they shall be ranked in order of their scores in the last race. Any remaining ties shall be broken by using the tied boats' scores in the next-to-last race and so on until all ties are broken. These scores shall be used even if some of them are excluded scores.

A9 RACE SCORES IN A SERIES LONGER THAN A REGATTA

For a series that is held over a period of time longer than a regatta, a boat that came to the starting area but did not *start*, did not *finish*, retired after *finishing* or was disqualified shall be scored points for the finishing place one more than the number of boats that came to the starting area. A boat that did not come to the starting area shall be scored points for the finishing place one more than the number of boats entered in the series.

A10 GUIDANCE ON REDRESS

If the protest committee decides to give redress by adjusting a boat's score for a race, it is advised to consider scoring her

(a) points equal to the average, to the nearest tenth of a point (0.05 to be rounded upward), of her points in all the races in the series except the race in question;

(b) points equal to the average, to the nearest tenth of a point (0.05 to be rounded upward), of her points in all the races before the race in question; or

(c) points based on the position of the boat in the race at the time of the incident that justified redress.

A11 SCORING ABBREVIATIONS

These abbreviations are recommended for recording the circumstances described:

DNC	Did not *start*; did not come to the starting area
DNS	Did not *start* (other than DNC and OCS)
OCS	Did not *start*; on the course side of the starting line at her starting signal and failed to *start*, or broke rule 30.1

ZFP	20% penalty under rule 30.2
BFD	Disqualification under rule 30.3
SCP	Took a scoring penalty under rule 44.3
DNF	Did not *finish*
RAF	Retired after *finishing*
DSQ	Disqualification
DNE	Disqualification (other than DGM) not excludable under rule 89.3(b)
DGM	Disqualification under rule 69.1(b)(2); not excludable
RDG	Redress given

APPENDIX B
WINDSURFING COMPETITION RULES

Windsurfing competition shall be sailed under The Racing Rules of Sailing *as changed by this appendix. The term 'boat' elsewhere in the racing rules means 'board' or 'boat' as appropriate. A windsurfing event can include one or more of the following disciplines or their formats:*

Discipline	Formats
Racing	*Course racing; slalom; marathon*
Expression	*Wave performance; freestyle*
Speed	

In expression competition a board's performance is judged on skill and variety rather than speed and is organized using elimination series. Either wave performance or freestyle competition is organized, depending on the wave conditions at the venue. In speed competition, a 'round' consists of one or more speed runs in which the boards take turns sailing the course at intervals. In the racing discipline a marathon race is a race scheduled to last more than one hour.

In slalom racing or expression competition, 'heat' means one elimination contest, a 'round' consists of one or more heats, and an elimination series consists of a maximum of four rounds.

B1 DEFINITIONS
B1.1 The following additional definitions apply:
Beach Start When the starting line is on the beach, or so close to the beach that the competitor must stand in the water to *start*, the start is a *beach start*.
Capsized A board is *capsized* when her sail or the competitor is in the water.

B1.2 The following definitions apply only to expression competition:

Coming In and Going Out A board sailing in the same direction as the incoming surf is *coming in*. A board sailing in the direction opposite to the incoming surf is *going out*.

Jumping A board is *jumping* when she takes off at the top of a wave while *going out*.

Overtaking A board is *overtaking* from the moment she gains an *overlap* from *clear astern* until the moment she is *clear ahead* of the *overtaken* board.

Possession The first board sailing shoreward immediately in front of a wave has *possession* of that wave. However, when it is impossible to determine which board is first the *windward* board has *possession*.

Recovering A board is *recovering* from the time her sail or, when water-starting, the competitor is out of the water until she has steerage way.

Surfing A board is *surfing* when she is on or immediately in front of a wave while *coming in*.

Transition A board changing *tacks*, or taking off while *coming in*, or one that is not *surfing*, *jumping*, *capsized* or *recovering* is in *transition*.

B2 RULES FOR ALL COMPETITION
B2.1 Changes to the Rules of Part 4
(a) Rule 42 is changed to 'A board shall be propelled only by the action of the wind on the sail, by the action of the water on the hull and by the unassisted actions of the competitor.'

(b) Add to rule 43.1(a): 'However, a competitor may wear a drinking container that shall have a capacity of at least one litre and weigh no more than 1.5 kilograms when full.'

(c) Rule 44.2 is changed so that two turns are replaced by one 360° turn with no requirement for tacks or gybes.

(d) Rules 44.3 and 44.4(a) are deleted.

(e) Add to rule 47.1: 'except as stated in rule 41.2'. (See rule B4.4.) Rule 47.2 is deleted.

B2.2 Entry and Qualification
Add to rule 78.1: 'When so prescribed by the ISAF, a numbered and dated device on a board and her centreboard, fin and rig shall serve as her measurement certificate.'

B2.3 Event Organization
(a) The last sentence of rule 89.2(c) is deleted.

(b) Add new rule 89.2(d): 'Oral instructions may be given only if the procedure is stated in the sailing instructions.'

B2.4 Identification on Sails
(a) Add to rule G1.1(a): 'The insignia shall not refer to anything other than the manufacturer or class and shall not consist of more than two letters and three numbers or an abstract design.'

(b) Rules G1.3(a), G1.3(c), G1.3(d) and G1.3(e) are changed to
The class insignia shall be displayed once on each side of the sail in the area above a line projected at right angles from a point on the luff of the sail one-third of the distance from the head to the wishbone. The national letters and sail numbers shall be in the central third of that part of the sail above the wishbone, clearly separated from any advertising, and placed at different heights on the two sides of the sail, those on the starboard side being uppermost.

B3 RULES FOR RACING COMPETITION
B3.1 When Boards Meet
(a) Rule 13 becomes rule 13.1. Add new rule 13.2:
A board gybing shall *keep clear* of other boards. During that time rules 10, 11 and 12 do not apply. If two boards are subject to this rule at the same time, the one on the other's port side or the one astern shall *keep clear*.

(b) Rules 17, 18.2(b), 18.2(c) and 18.3 are deleted.

(c) Rule 21 becomes rule 21.1. Add new rule 21.2: 'A *capsized* board shall not take an action that hinders another board.'

(d) Add new rule 22.3: 'A board shall not sail in the course area defined in the sailing instructions when races are taking place except in her own race.'

(e) Add new rule 23:
23 SAIL OUT OF THE WATER WHEN STARTING
When approaching the starting line to *start*, a board shall have her sail out of the water and in a normal position, except when accidentally *capsized*.

B3.2 Starting Races
The sailing instructions shall specify one of these starting systems.

(a) SYSTEM 1
See rule 26, Starting Races.

(b) SYSTEM 2

Races shall be started by using the following signals. Times shall be taken from the visual signals; the absence of a sound signal shall be disregarded.

Signal	Flag and sound	Minutes before starting signal
Attention	Class flag or heat number	5
	Attention signal removed	4
Warning	Red flag; 1 sound	3
	Red flag removed	2
Preparatory	Yellow flag; 1 sound	1
	Yellow flag removed	1/2
Starting	Green flag; 1 sound	0

(c) SYSTEM 3 (FOR BEACH STARTS)

(1) Before her start each board in a heat or class shall draw a number for her station on the starting line. The stations shall be numbered so that station 1 is the most windward one.
(2) After boards have been called to take their positions, the race committee shall make the preparatory signal by displaying a red flag with one sound. The starting signal shall be made, at any time after the preparatory signal, by removing the red flag with one sound.
(3) After the starting signal each board shall take the shortest route from her starting station to her windsurfing position on the water (with both of the competitor's feet on the board).

B3.3 Other Rules for the Conduct of a Race
(a) Add new rule 29.3:
29.3 Recall for a Slalom Race
(a) When at a board's starting signal for a slalom race or heat any part of her hull, crew or equipment is on the course side of the starting line, the race committee shall signal a general recall.
(b) If the race committee acts under rule 29.3(a) and the board is identified, she shall be disqualified without a hearing, even if the race or heat is *postponed* or *abandoned*. The race committee shall hail or display her sail number, and she shall leave the course area immediately. If the race or heat is restarted or resailed, she shall not sail in it.

(b) Change rule 31 to 'A board may touch a *mark* but shall not hold on to it.'

B4 RULES FOR EXPRESSION COMPETITION
B4.1 Right-of-Way Rules
These rules replace all rules of Part 2.

(a) COMING IN AND GOING OUT

A board *coming in* shall *keep clear* of a board *going out*. When two boards are *going out* or *coming in* while on the same wave, or when neither is *going out* or *coming in*, the board on *port tack* shall *keep clear* of the one on *starboard tack*.

(b) BOARDS ON THE SAME WAVE, COMING IN

When two or more boards are on a wave *coming in*, a board that does not have *possession* shall *keep clear*.

(c) CLEAR ASTERN, CLEAR AHEAD AND OVERTAKING

A board *clear astern* and not on a wave shall *keep clear* of a board *clear ahead*. An *overtaking* board that is not on a wave shall *keep clear*.

(d) TRANSITION

A board in *transition* shall *keep clear* of one that is not. When two boards are in *transition* at the same time, the one on the other's port side or the one astern shall *keep clear*.

B4.2 Starting and Ending Heats
Heats shall be started and ended by using the following signals:

(a) STARTING A HEAT

Each flag shall be removed when the next flag is displayed.

Signal	Flag and sound	Minutes before starting signal
Attention	Heat number	3
Warning	Red flag; 1 sound	2
Preparatory	Yellow flag; 1 sound	1
Starting	Green flag; 1 sound	0

(b) ENDING A HEAT

Signal	Flag and sound	Minutes before ending signal
End warning	Green flag removed; 1 sound	1
Ending	Red flag; 1 sound	0

B4.3 Registration of Sails; Course Area; Heat Duration
(a) Boards shall register with the race committee the colours and other particulars of their sails, or their identification according to another method stated in the sailing instructions, no later than the starting signal for the heat two heats before their own.

(b) The course area shall be defined in the sailing instructions and posted on the official notice board not later than 30 minutes before the starting signal for the first heat. A board shall be scored only while sailing in the course area.

(c) Any change in heat duration shall be announced by the race committee not later than fifteen minutes before the starting signal for the first heat in the next round.

B4.4 Outside Help
Rule 41 becomes rule 41.1. Add new rule 41.2:
An assistant may provide replacement equipment to a board but shall keep clear of other boards competing. A board whose assistant fails to keep clear shall be penalized. The penalty shall be at the discretion of the protest committee.

B5 ELIMINATION SERIES FOR SLALOM RACING AND EXPRESSION COMPETITION
Rules B5.1–B5.5 apply to slalom racing or expression competition organized by using elimination series in which boards compete in heats.

B5.1 Elimination Series Procedure
(a) Competition shall take the form of one or more elimination series. Each of them shall consist of either a maximum of four rounds in a single elimination series where only a number of the best scorers advance, or a maximum of ten rounds in a double elimination series where boards have more than one opportunity to advance.

(b) Boards shall sail one against another in pairs, or in groups determined by the elimination ladder. The selected form of competition shall not be changed while a round remains uncompleted.

B5.2 Seeding and Ranking Lists
(a) When a seeding or ranking list is used to establish the heats of the first round, places 1–8 (four heats) or 1–16 (eight heats) shall be distributed evenly among the heats.

(b) For a subsequent elimination series, if any, boards shall be reassigned to new heats according to a seeding list based on the current overall standings.

(c) The organizing authority's seeding decisions are final and are not grounds for a request for redress.

B5.3 Heat Schedule
The schedule of heats shall be posted on the official notice board not later than 30 minutes before the starting signal for the first heat.

B5.4 Advancement and Byes
(a) In slalom racing and freestyle competition, the boards in each heat to advance to the next round shall be announced by the race committee not later than 30 minutes before the starting signal for the first heat. The number advancing may be changed by the protest committee as a result of a redress decision.

(b) In expression competition, any first-round byes shall be assigned to the highest-seeded boards.

(c) In wave performance competition, only the winner of each heat shall advance to the next round.

(d) In freestyle competition, boards shall advance to the next round as follows: from an eight-board heat, the best four advance, and the winner will sail against the fourth and the second against the third; from a four-board heat, the best two advance and will sail against each other.

B5.5 Finals
(a) The final shall consist of a maximum of three races. The race committee shall announce the number of races to be sailed in the final not later than five minutes before the warning signal for the first final race.

(b) A runners-up final may be sailed after the final. All boards in the semifinal heats that failed to qualify for the final may compete in it.

B6 RULES FOR SPEED COMPETITION

B6.1 General Rules
All rules of Part 2 are replaced by relevant parts of this rule.

(a) BEACH AND WATER STARTING

A board shall not *beach start* or water start on the course or in the starting area, except to sail off the course to avoid boards that are *starting* or *racing*.

(b) LEAVING THE COURSE AREA

A board leaving the course area shall *keep clear* of boards *racing*.

(c) COURSE CONTROL

When the race committee points an orange flag at a board, she shall immediately leave the course area.

(d) RETURNING TO THE STARTING AREA

A board returning to the starting area shall keep clear of the course.

(e) RUN; ROUND

The maximum number of runs to be made by each board in a round shall be announced by the race committee not later than 30 minutes before the starting signal for the first round.

(f) DURATION OF A ROUND

The duration of a round shall be announced by the race committee not later than 30 minutes before the starting signal for the next round.

(g) CONDITIONS FOR ESTABLISHING A RECORD

The minimum distance for a world record is 500 metres. Other records may be established over shorter distances. The course shall be defined by posts and transits ashore or by buoys afloat. Transits shall not converge.

B6.2 Starting System for Speed Competition
Rounds shall be started and ended by using the following signals. Each flag shall be removed when the next flag is displayed.

(a) STARTING A ROUND

Signal	Flag	Meaning
Stand-by	Red flag	Course closed
Course closed	AP and red flag	Course closed; will open shortly
Preparatory	Yellow flag	Course will open in 5 minutes
Starting	Green flag	Course is open

(b) ENDING A ROUND

Signal	Flag	Meaning
End warning	Green and yellow flag	Course will be closed in 5 minutes
Extension	Green flag and L	Current round extended by 15 minutes
Round ended	Red flag and L	A new round will be started shortly

B6.3 Penalties
(a) If a board fails to comply with a warning by the race committee, she may be cautioned and her sail number shall be posted on a notice board near the finishing line.

(b) If a board is cautioned a second time during the same round, she shall be suspended by the race committee from the remainder of the round and her sail number shall be posted on the official notice board.

(c) A board observed in the course area while suspended shall be disqualified from the competition without a hearing and none of her previous times or results shall be valid.

(d) Any breach of the verification rules may result in a suspension from the competition for any period.

B6.4 Verification
(a) An observer appointed by the World Sailing Speed Record Council (WSSRC) shall be present and verify run times and speeds at world record attempts. The race committee shall verify run times and speeds at other record attempts.

(b) A competitor shall not enter the timing control area or discuss any timing matter directly with the timing organization. Any timing question shall be directed to the race committee.

B7 PROTESTS, REDRESS, HEARINGS AND APPEALS
B7.1 (a) Add after the third sentence of rule 61.1(a): 'She shall inform the race committee of her intention to protest immediately after she *finishes* or retires.'

(b) Rule 61.2 is retitled rule 61.2(a), Course and Marathon Racing. Add new rule 61.2(b):

SLALOM RACING AND OTHER DISCIPLINES
A *protest* shall be made orally immediately following the heat
in which the incident occurred.

B7.2 Add new rule 62.1(e): 'a board that failed to *keep clear*
and retired or was penalized.'

B7.3 In rule 62.2, after 'writing' add: 'except in an elimination
series'.

B7.4 Rule 63.2 becomes rule 63.2(a). Add new rule 63.2(b):
'In an elimination series, the protest committee may hear a
protest on the beach or water immediately after the heat.'

B7.5 Begin rule 65.2 with the addition 'Except in an
elimination series'.

B7.6 Rule 67 is deleted.

B7.7 Add new rule 70.6: 'Appeals are not permitted in slalom
racing and expression competition.'

B8 SCORING
B8.1 Overall Scores
If an event includes more than one discipline or format
the sailing instructions shall state how the overall score
is to be calculated.

B8.2 Series Scores
Rule A2 is changed to
Each board's series score shall be the total of her race,
elimination series or speed round scores with the number
of her worst scores excluded as follows:

Course races, speed rounds	Slalom and expression elimination series	Number excluded
1–3	1–2	0
4–6	3–4	1
7–10	5–7	2
11–15	8 or more	3
16 or more		4

If a board has two or more equal worst scores, the score(s) for
the race(s) sailed earliest in the series shall be excluded. The
board with the lowest series score wins and others shall be
ranked accordingly. Rules B8.5, B8.6 and B8.7 contain
exceptions to this rule.

B8.3 Scoring Systems
(a) Rule A4 is retitled 'Low Point and Alternative Systems' and
its preamble is deleted. Rule A4.1 is changed to
Each board *starting* and *finishing* and not thereafter retiring,
being penalized or given redress shall be scored points as
follows:

Finishing place	Low Point System	Alternative System
First	1	0.7
Second	2	2
Third	3	3
Each place thereafter	Add 1 point	Add 1 point

(b) Add to the end of the first sentence of rule A4.2: 'or, in an
elimination series, the number of boards in that heat'.

B8.4 Uncompleted Heat
When a heat cannot be completed, the points for the
unscored places shall be added together and divided by the
number of places in that heat. The resulting number of points,
to the nearest tenth of a point (0.05 to be rounded upward),
shall be given to each board entered in the heat.

B8.5 Scoring a Final Series in Slalom
(a) If three final races are completed, a board's series score in
the final shall be the total of her race scores excluding her
worst score. Otherwise her series score shall be the total of

her race scores.

(b) A board that did not *start*, did not *finish*, retired after
finishing or was disqualified from a final race shall be scored
points equal to the total number of boards entered in the final.

B8.6 Expression Competition Scoring
(a) Expression competition shall be scored by a panel of
three judges. However, the panel may have a greater odd
number of members, and there may be two such panels. Each
judge shall give points for each manoeuvre based on the
scale stated in the sailing instructions.

(b) The criteria of scoring shall be decided by the race
committee and announced on the official notice board
not later than 30 minutes before the starting signal for the
first heat.

(c) A board's heat standing shall be determined by adding
together the points given by each judge. The board with the
highest score wins and others shall be ranked accordingly.

(d) Both semifinal heats shall have been sailed for an
elimination series to be valid.

(e) Except for members of the race committee responsible
for scoring the event, only competitors in the heat shall be
allowed to see judges' score sheets for the heat. Each score
sheet shall bear the full name of the judge.

(f) Scoring decisions of the judges shall not be grounds for
a request for redress by a board.

B8.7 Speed Competition
The speeds of a board's fastest two runs in a round shall be
averaged to determine her standing in that round. The board
with the highest average wins and others shall be ranked
accordingly.

B8.8 Series Ties
(a) RACING AND SPEED COMPETITION

Rule A8 is changed as follows for racing and speed
competition:
(1) Add new rule A8.1: 'If there is a series score tie between
two or more boards, it shall be broken in favour of the
board(s) with the best single excluded race score(s).'
(2) Rule A8.1 becomes rule A8.2. Its beginning 'If there is a
series score tie' is changed to 'If a tie remains' and its last
sentence is changed to 'These scores shall be used even if
some of them are excluded scores.'
(3) Rule A8.2 becomes rule A8.3 and its beginning 'If a tie
remains' is changed to 'If a tie still remains'.

(b) EXPRESSION COMPETITION

Rule A8 is changed as follows for expression competition:
(1) In a heat, if there is a tie in the total points given by
one or more judges, it shall be broken in favour of the
board with the higher single score in the priority category.
If the categories are weighted equally, in wave
performance competition the tie shall be broken in favour
of the board with the higher single score in wave riding,
and in freestyle competition in favour of the board with
the higher score for overall impression. If a tie remains,
in wave performance competition it shall be broken in
favour of the board with the higher single score in the
category without priority, and in freestyle competition it
shall stand as the final result.
(2) If there is a tie in the series score, it shall be broken
in favour of the board that scored better more times than
the other board. All scores shall be used even if some of
them are excluded scores.
(3) If a tie still remains, the heat shall be resailed. If this is
not possible, the tie shall stand as the final result.

APPENDIX C
MATCH RACING RULES

Match races shall be sailed under The Racing Rules of Sailing *as changed by this appendix. Matches shall be umpired unless the notice of race and sailing instructions state otherwise.*

C1 TERMINOLOGY
'Competitor' means the skipper, team or boat as appropriate for the event. 'Flight' means two or more matches started in the same starting sequence.

C2 CHANGES TO THE DEFINITIONS AND THE RULES OF PARTS 2 AND 4
C2.1 The definition *Finish* is changed to
A boat *finishes* when any part of her hull, or crew or equipment in normal position, crosses the finishing line in the direction of the course from the last *mark* after completing any penalties. However, when penalties are cancelled under rule C7.2(d) after one or both boats have *finished* each shall be recorded as *finished* when she crossed the line.

C2.2 Add to the definition *Proper Course*: 'A boat taking a penalty or manoeuvring to take a penalty is not sailing a *proper course.*'

C2.3 The last sentence of the definition *Clear Ahead* and *Clear Astern; Overlap* is changed to 'These terms do not apply to boats on opposite *tacks* unless either rule 18 applies or both boats are subject to rule 13.2.'

C2.4 Rule 13 is changed to

13 WHILE TACKING OR GYBING
13.1 After a boat passes head to wind, she shall *keep clear* of other boats until she is on a close-hauled course.

13.2 After the foot of the mainsail of a boat sailing downwind crosses the centreline she shall *keep clear* of other boats until her mainsail has filled.

13.3 While rule 13.1 or 13.2 applies, rules 10, 11 and 12 do not. However, if two boats are subject to rule 13.1 or 13.2 at the same time, the one on the other's port side or the one astern shall *keep clear.*

C2.5 Rules 16.2 and 17.2 are deleted.

C2.6 Rule 18.3 is changed to
If two boats were on opposite *tacks* and one of them completes a tack within the *two-length zone* to pass a rounding *mark*, and if thereafter the other boat cannot by luffing avoid becoming *overlapped* inside her, the boat that tacked shall *keep clear* and rules 15 and 18.2 do not apply. If the other boat can by luffing avoid becoming *overlapped* inside her then rule 18.2(c) shall apply as if the boats were *clear ahead* and *clear astern* at the *two-length zone.*

C2.7 When rule 19.1 applies, the following arm signals by the helmsman are required in addition to the hails:

(a) for 'Room to tack', repeatedly and clearly pointing to windward; and

(b) for 'You tack', repeatedly and clearly pointing at the other boat and waving the arm to windward.

C2.8 Rule 20.2 is changed to 'A boat taking a penalty shall *keep clear* of one that is not.'

C2.9 Rule 22.1 is changed to 'If reasonably possible, a boat not *racing* shall not interfere with a boat that is *racing* or an umpire boat.'

C2.10 Rule 22.2 is changed to 'Except when sailing a *proper course*, a boat shall not interfere with a boat taking a penalty or sailing on another leg.'

C2.11 Add new rule 22.3: 'When boats in different matches meet, any change of course by either boat shall be consistent with complying with a *rule* or trying to win her own match.'

C2.12 Add to the preamble of Part 4: 'Rule 42 shall also apply between the warning and preparatory signals.'

C2.13 Rule 42.2(d) is changed to 'sculling: repeated movement of the helm to propel the boat forward;'.

C3 RACE SIGNALS AND CHANGES TO RELATED RULES
C3.1 Starting Signals
The signals for starting a match shall be as follows. Times shall be taken from the visual signals; the failure of a sound signal shall be disregarded. If more than one match will be sailed, the starting signal for one match shall be the warning signal for the next match.

Time in minutes	Visual signal	Sound signal	Means
10	Flag F displayed	One	Attention signal
6	Flag F removed	None	
5	Numeral pennant displayed*	One	Warning signal
4	Flag P displayed	One	Preparatory signal
2	Blue or yellow flag or both displayed**	One**	End of pre-start entry time
0	Warning and preparatory signals removed	One	Starting signal

* Within a flight, numeral pennant 1 means Match 1, pennant 2 means Match 2, etc., unless the sailing instructions state otherwise.
** These signals shall be made only if one or both boats fail to comply with rule C4.2. The flag(s) shall be displayed until the umpires have signalled a penalty or for one minute, whichever is earlier.

C3.2 Changes to Related Rules
(a) Rule 29.1 is changed to
(1) When at a boat's starting signal any part of her hull, crew or equipment is on the course side of the starting line or its extensions, the race committee shall promptly display a blue or yellow flag identifying the boat with one sound. The flag shall be displayed until the boat is completely on the pre-start side of the starting line or its extensions or until two minutes after her starting signal, whichever is earlier.
(2) When at a boat's starting signal no part of her hull, crew or equipment is on the course side of the starting line or its extensions, and before she *starts* she sails to the course side across an extension, the race committee shall promptly display a blue or yellow flag identifying the boat. The flag shall be displayed until the boat is completely on the pre-start side of the starting line or its extensions or until two minutes after her starting signal, whichever is earlier.

(b) In the race signal AP the last sentence is changed to 'The attention signal will be made 1 minute after removal unless at that time the race is *postponed* again or *abandoned.*'

(c) In the race signal N the last sentence is changed to 'The attention signal will be made 1 minute after removal unless at that time the race is *abandoned* again or *postponed.*'

C3.3 Finishing Line Signals
The race signal Blue flag or shape shall not be used.

C4 REQUIREMENTS BEFORE THE START
C4.1 At her preparatory signal, each boat shall be outside the line that is at a 90° angle to the starting line through the starting *mark* at her assigned end. In the race schedule

pairing list, the boat listed on the left-hand side is assigned the port end and shall display a blue flag at her stern while *racing*. The other boat is assigned the starboard end and shall display a yellow flag at her stern while *racing*.

C4.2 Within the two-minute period following her preparatory signal, a boat shall cross and clear the starting line, the first time from the course side to the pre-start side.

C5 SIGNALS BY UMPIRES
C5.1 A green and white flag with one long sound means 'No penalty.'

C5.2 A blue or yellow flag identifying a boat with one long sound means 'The identified boat shall take a penalty by complying with rule C7.'

C5.3 A red flag with or soon after a blue or yellow flag with one long sound means 'The identified boat shall take a penalty by complying with rule C7.3(d).'

C5.4 A black flag with a blue or yellow flag and one long sound means 'The identified boat is disqualified, and the match is terminated and awarded to the other boat.'

C5.5 One short sound means 'A penalty is now completed.'

C5.6 Repetitive short sounds mean 'A boat is no longer taking a penalty and the penalty remains.'

C5.7 A blue or yellow flag or shape displayed from an umpire boat means 'The identified boat has an outstanding penalty.'

C6 PROTESTS AND REQUESTS FOR REDRESS BY BOATS
C6.1 A boat may protest another boat

(a) under a rule of Part 2, except rule 14, by clearly displaying flag Y immediately after an incident in which she was involved;

(b) under any rule not listed in rule C6.1(a) or C6.2 by clearly displaying a red flag as soon as possible after the incident.

C6.2 A boat may not protest another boat under
(a) rule 14, unless damage or injury results;

(b) a rule of Part 2, unless she was involved in the incident;

(c) rule 31 or 42; or

(d) rule C4 or C7.

C6.3 A boat intending to request redress because of circumstances that arise before she *finishes* or retires shall clearly display a red flag as soon as possible after she becomes aware of those circumstances, but not later than two minutes after *finishing* or retiring.

C6.4 (a) A boat protesting under rule C6.1(a) shall remove flag Y before or as soon as possible after the umpires' signal.

(b) A boat protesting under rule C6.1(b) or requesting redress under rule C6.3 shall, for her *protest* or request to be valid, keep her red flag displayed until she has so informed the umpires after *finishing* or retiring. No written *protest* or request for redress is required.

C6.5 Umpire Decisions
(a) After flag Y is displayed, the umpires shall decide whether to penalize any boat. They shall signal their decision in compliance with rule C5.1, C5.2 or C5.3.

(b) The red-flag penalty in rule C5.3 shall be used when a boat has gained control as a result of breaking a *rule*, but the umpires are not certain that the conditions for an additional

umpire-initiated penalty have been fulfilled.

C6.6 Protest Committee Decisions
(a) The protest committee may take evidence in any way it considers appropriate and may communicate its decision orally.

(b) If the protest committee decides that a breach of a *rule* has had no significant effect on the outcome of the match, it may
(1) impose a penalty of one point or part of one point;
(2) order a resail; or
(3) make another arrangement it decides is equitable, which may be to impose no penalty.

(c) The penalty for breaking rule 14 when damage or injury results will be at the discretion of the protest committee, and may include exclusion from further races in the event.

C7 PENALTY SYSTEM
C7.1 Rule Changes
Rules 31.2 and 44 are deleted.

C7.2 All Penalties
(a) A penalized boat may delay taking a penalty within the limitations of rule C7.3 and shall take it as follows:
(1) When on a leg of the course to a windward *mark*, she shall gybe and, as soon as reasonably possible, luff to a close-hauled course.
(2) When on a leg of the course to a leeward *mark* or the finishing line, she shall tack and, as soon as reasonably possible, bear away to a downwind course.

(b) Add to rule 2: 'When *racing*, a boat may wait for an umpire's decision before taking a penalty.'

(c) A boat completes a leg of the course when her bow crosses the extension of the line from the previous *mark* through the *mark* she is rounding, or on the last leg when she *finishes*.

(d) A penalized boat shall not be recorded as having *finished* until she takes her penalty and sails completely to the course side of the line and then *finishes*, unless the penalty is cancelled before or after she crosses the finishing line.

(e) If a boat has one or two outstanding penalties and the other boat in her match is penalized, one penalty for each boat shall be cancelled except that a red-flag penalty shall not cancel an outstanding penalty.

(f) If a boat has more than two outstanding penalties, the umpires shall signal her disqualification under rule C5.4.

C7.3 Penalty Limitations
(a) A boat taking a penalty that includes a tack shall have the spinnaker head below the main-boom gooseneck from the time she passes head to wind until she is on a close-hauled course.

(b) No part of a penalty may be taken within two of a boat's hull lengths of a rounding *mark*.

(c) If a boat has one outstanding penalty, she may take the penalty any time after *starting* and before *finishing*. If a boat has two outstanding penalties, she shall take one of them as soon as reasonably possible, but not before *starting*.

(d) When the umpires display a red flag with or soon after a penalty flag, the penalized boat shall take a penalty as soon as reasonably possible, but not before *starting*.

C7.4 Taking and Completing Penalties
(a) When a boat with an outstanding penalty is on a leg to a windward *mark* and gybes, or is on a leg to a leeward *mark* or the finishing line and passes head to wind, she is taking a penalty.

(b) When a boat taking a penalty either does not take the penalty correctly or does not complete the penalty as soon as reasonably possible, she is no longer taking a penalty. The umpires shall signal this as required by rule C5.6.

(c) The umpire boat for each match shall display blue or yellow flags or shapes, each flag or shape indicating one outstanding penalty. When a boat has taken a penalty, or a penalty has been cancelled, one flag or shape shall be removed. Failure of the umpires to display or remove flags or shapes shall not change the number of penalties outstanding.

C8 PENALTIES INITIATED BY UMPIRES
C8.1 Rule Changes
(a) Rules 60.2(a) and 60.3(a) do not apply to *rules* for which penalties may be imposed by umpires.

(b) Rule 64.1(b) is changed so that the provision for exonerating a boat may be applied by the umpires without a hearing, and it takes precedence over any conflicting rule of this appendix.

C8.2 When the umpires decide that a boat has broken rule 31, 42, C4, C7.3(c) or C7.3(d) she shall be penalized by signalling her under rule C5.2 or C5.3. However, a boat that displays an incorrect flag or does not display the correct flag shall be warned orally and given an opportunity to correct the error before being penalized.

C8.3 When the umpires decide that a boat has
(a) gained an advantage by breaking a *rule* after allowing for a penalty,

(b) deliberately broken a *rule*, or

(c) committed a breach of sportsmanship,
she shall be penalized under rule C5.2, C5.3 or C5.4.

C8.4 If the umpires or protest committee members decide that a boat may have broken a *rule* other than those listed in rules C6.1(a) and C6.2, they shall so inform the protest committee for its action under rule 60.3 and rule C6.6 when appropriate.

C8.5 When, after one boat has *started*, the umpires are satisfied that the other boat will not *start*, they may signal under rule C5.4 that the boat that did not *start* is disqualified and the match is terminated.

C9 REQUESTS FOR REDRESS OR REOPENING; APPEALS; OTHER PROCEEDINGS
C9.1 There shall be no request for redress or an appeal from a decision made under rule C5, C6, C7 or C8. In rule 66 the third sentence is changed to 'A *party* to the hearing may not ask for a reopening.'

C9.2 A competitor may not base a request for redress on a claim that an action by an official boat was improper. The protest committee may decide to consider giving redress in such circumstances but only if it believes that an official boat, including an umpire boat, may have seriously interfered with a competing boat.

C9.3 No proceedings of any kind may be taken in relation to any action or non-action by the umpires, except as permitted in rule C9.2.

C10 SCORING
C10.1 The winning competitor of each match scores one point (half of one point each for a dead heat); the loser scores no points.

C10.2 When a competitor withdraws from part of an event the scores of all completed races shall stand.

C10.3 When a multiple round robin is terminated with an incomplete round robin, only one point shall be available for all the matches sailed between any two competitors, as follows:

Number of matches completed between any two competitors	Points for each win
1	One point
2	One-half point
3	One-third point
(etc.)	

C10.4 In a round-robin series,
(a) competitors shall be placed in order of their total scores, highest score first;

(b) a competitor who has won a match but is disqualified for breaking a *rule* against a competitor in another match shall lose the point for that match (but the losing competitor shall not be awarded the point); and

(c) the overall position between competitors who have sailed in different groups shall be decided by the highest score.

C10.5 In a knockout series the sailing instructions shall state the minimum number of points required to win a series between two competitors. When a knockout series is terminated it shall be decided in favour of the competitor with the higher score.

C11 TIES
C11.1 Round-Robin Series
A round-robin series means a grouping of competitors who all sail against each other one or more times. Each separate stage identified in the event format shall be a separate round-robin series irrespective of the number of times each competitor sails against each other competitor in that stage.

Ties between two or more competitors in a round-robin series shall be broken by the following methods, in order, until all ties are broken. When one or more ties are only partially broken, rules C11.1(a) to C11.1(e) shall be reapplied to them. Ties shall be decided in favour of the competitor(s) who

(a) placed in order, has the highest score in the matches between the tied competitors.

(b) when the tie is between two competitors in a multiple round robin, has won the last match between the two competitors.

(c) has the most points against the competitor placed highest in the round-robin series or, if necessary, second highest, and so on until the tie is broken. When two separate ties have to be resolved but the resolution of each depends upon resolving the other, the following principles shall be used in the rule C11.1(c) procedure:
(1) the higher-place tie shall be resolved before the lower-place tie, and
(2) all the competitors in the lower-place tie shall be treated as a single competitor for the purposes of rule C11.1(c).

(d) after applying rule C10.4(c), has the highest place in the different groups, irrespective of the number of competitors in each group.

(e) has the highest place in the most recent stage of the event (fleet race, round robin, etc.).

C11.2 Knockout Series
Ties (including 0–0) between two competitors in a knockout series shall be broken by the following methods, in order, until the tie is broken. The tie shall be decided in favour of the competitor who

(a) has the highest place in the most recent round-robin series, applying rule C11.1 if necessary;

(b) has won the most recent match in the event between the tied competitors.

C11.3 Remaining Ties
When rule C11.1 or C11.2 does not resolve a tie,

(a) if the tie needs to be resolved for a later stage of the event (or another event for which the event is a direct qualifier), the tie shall be broken by a sail-off when practicable. When the race committee decides a sail-off is not practicable the tie shall be broken by a draw.

(b) to decide the winner of an event that is not a direct qualifier for another event, or the overall position between competitors eliminated in one round of a knockout series, a sail-off may be used (but not a draw).

(c) when a tie is not broken any monetary prizes or ranking points for tied places shall be added together and divided equally among the tied competitors.

Note: A Standard Notice of Race and Standard Sailing Instructions for match racing are available from the ISAF.

APPENDIX D
TEAM RACING RULES

Team races shall be sailed under The Racing Rules of Sailing *as changed by this appendix. If umpires will be used the sailing instructions shall so state.*

D1 CHANGES TO THE RACING RULES
D1.1 Changes to the Rules of Part 2
(a) Rule 17.2 is changed to 'Except on a beat to windward, while a boat is less than two of her hull lengths from a *leeward* boat, she shall not sail below her *proper course* unless she gybes.'

(b) The first sentence of rule 18.2(c) is changed to 'If a boat was *clear ahead* at the time she reached the *two-length zone*, or she later became *clear ahead* when another boat passed head to wind, the boat *clear astern* shall thereafter *keep clear*.'

(c) Rule 18.4 is deleted.

(d) Add new rule 22.3: 'A boat that has *finished* shall not act to interfere with a boat that has not *finished*.'

(e) Add new rule 22.4: 'When boats in different races meet, any change of course by either boat shall be consistent with complying with a *rule* or trying to win her own race.'

D1.2 Other Additional Rules
(a) There shall be no penalty for breaking a rule of Part 2 when the incident is between boats on the same team and there is no contact.

(b) Add to rule 41: 'However, a boat may receive help from another boat on her team provided electronic communication is not used.'

(c) A boat is not eligible for redress based on damage or injury caused by another boat on her team.

D2 PROTESTS AND PENALTIES
D2.1 Protests and Exoneration
(a)The third sentence of rule 61.1(a) and all of rule 61.1(a)(2) are deleted.

(b) A boat that, while *racing*, may have broken a rule of Part 2 (except rule 14 when she has caused damage or injury) or rule 42 may take a penalty complying with rule 44.2, except that only one turn is required.

(c) The sailing instructions may state that rule D2.4(b) applies

to all *protests*.

D2.2 Umpired Races
Races to be umpired shall be identified either in the sailing instructions or by the display of flag U no later than the warning signal.

(a) When a boat protests under a rule of Part 2 or under rule 31.1, 42 or 44, she is not entitled to a hearing, except under rule 14 when there is damage or injury. Instead, when the protested boat fails either to acknowledge breaking a *rule* or to take the appropriate penalty, the protesting boat may request a decision by conspicuously displaying a yellow flag and hailing 'Umpire'.

(b) An umpire shall signal a decision as follows:
(1) A green flag or a green and white flag means 'No penalty'.
(2) A red flag means 'One or more boats are penalized.' The umpire shall hail or signal to identify each boat to be penalized.

(c) A boat penalized under rule D2.2(b)(2) shall take a Two-Turns Penalty under rule 44.2.

(d) PENALTIES INITIATED BY UMPIRES

When a boat
(1) breaks rule 31.1 or 42, or a rule of Part 2 through contact with another boat on her team, and does not take a penalty;
(2) fails to comply with rule D2.2(c);
(3) commits a breach of sportsmanship; or
(4) breaks rule 14 when damage or injury may have been caused;
or when a boat or her team gains an advantage despite taking a penalty, an umpire may take action without a *protest* from another boat. The umpire may impose a penalty of one or more turns, each including one tack and one gybe, signalled by displaying a red flag and hailing the boat accordingly, or report the incident to the protest committee, signalled by displaying a black flag, or both.

D2.3 Alternative Umpiring Rules
Each of these rules applies only if the sailing instructions so state.

(a) SINGLE-FLAG PROTEST PROCEDURE

Rule D2.2(a) is replaced by
When a boat protests under a rule of Part 2 or under rule 31.1, 42 or 44, she is not entitled to a hearing, except under rule 14 when there is damage or injury. Instead, a boat involved in the incident may promptly acknowledge breaking a *rule* and take the appropriate penalty. If no boat takes a penalty, an umpire shall decide whether any boat has broken a *rule*, and shall signal the decision in compliance with rule D2.2(b).

(b) RACES WITH LIMITED UMPIRING

Rule D2.2 applies, except that when a boat complies with rule D2.2(a) and either there is no decision signalled or an umpire displays a yellow flag signalling he has insufficient facts to decide, the protesting boat is entitled to a hearing.

D2.4 Additional Protest and Redress Rules When Races Are Umpired
(a) Neither the race committee nor the protest committee shall protest a boat for breaking a rule listed in rule D2.2(a), except under rule 14 when there is damage or injury.

(b) *Protests* and requests for redress need not be in writing.

The protest committee may take evidence in any way it considers appropriate and may communicate its decision orally.

(c) There shall be no request for redress or appeal by a boat arising from a decision, action or non-action by an umpire. The protest committee may decide to consider giving redress when it believes that an official boat, including an umpire boat, may have seriously interfered with a competing boat.

D3 SCORING A RACE

D3.1 (a) Each boat *finishing* a race, whether or not rule 28.1 has been complied with, shall be scored points equal to her finishing place. All other boats shall be scored points equal to the number of boats entitled to *race*.

(b) In addition, a boat's points shall be increased as follows:

Rule broken	Penalty points
Rule 28.1 when as a result she or her team has gained an advantage	10
Any other *rule* broken while *racing* for which a penalty has not been taken	6

(c) After a hearing the protest committee may penalize as follows:
(1) When a boat has broken a *rule* and as a result her team has gained an advantage, it may increase that boat's points.
(2) When a boat has broken rule 1 or 2, rule 14 when she has caused damage or injury, or a *rule* when not *racing*, it may penalize the boat's team by half or more race wins, or it may impose no penalty.

(d) The team with the lower total points wins the race. If the totals are equal, the team that did not have the first-place boat wins.

D3.2 When all boats on one team have *finished*, retired or failed to *start*, the race committee may stop the race. The other team's boats *racing* at that time shall be scored the points they would have received had they *finished*.

D4 SCORING A SERIES

D4.1 When two or more teams are competing in a series, the winner shall be the team scoring the greatest number of race wins. The other teams shall be ranked in order of number of race wins.

D4.2 When necessary, ties in a completed series shall be broken using, in order,

(a) the number of races won when the tied teams met;

(b) the points scored when the tied teams met;

(c) if two teams remain tied, the last race between them;

(d) total points scored in all races against common opponents;

(e) a sail-off if possible, otherwise a game of chance.
If a multiple tie is only partially resolved by one of these, then the remaining tie shall be broken by starting again at rule D4.2(a).

D4.3 If a series is not completed, teams shall be ranked according to the results from completed rounds, and ties shall be broken whenever possible using the results from races between the tied teams in the incomplete round. If no round has been completed, teams shall be ranked in order of their percentages of races won. Other ties shall be broken as provided in rule D4.2.

D5 BREAKDOWNS WHEN BOATS ARE SUPPLIED BY THE ORGANIZING AUTHORITY

D5.1 A supplied boat suffering a breakdown, and seeking redress as a result, shall display a red flag at the first reasonable opportunity and, if possible, continue *racing*. The race committee shall decide redress as provided in rules D5.2 and D5.3.

D5.2 When the race committee decides that the boat's finishing position was made significantly worse, that the breakdown was through no fault of the crew, and that in the same circumstances a reasonably competent crew would not have been able to avoid the breakdown, it shall make as equitable a decision as possible. This may be to order the race to be resailed or, when the boat's finishing position was predictable, award her points for that position. Any doubt about a boat's position when she broke down shall be resolved against her.

D5.3 A breakdown caused by defective supplied equipment or a breach of a *rule* by an opponent shall not normally be determined to be the fault of the crew, but one caused by careless handling, capsizing or a breach by a boat on the same team shall be. Any doubt about the fault of the crew shall be resolved in the boat's favour.

APPENDIX E
RADIO-CONTROLLED BOAT RACING RULES

Races for radio-controlled boats shall be sailed under The Racing Rules of Sailing *as changed by this appendix.*

E1 TERMINOLOGY, RACE SIGNALS, DEFINITIONS AND FUNDAMENTAL RULES

E1.1 Terminology
'Boat' means a boat that is radio-controlled by a competitor who is not on board. For 'race' used as a noun outside this appendix and outside Appendix A read 'heat'. Within this appendix, a race consists of one or more heats and is completed when the last heat in the race is finished. An 'event' consists of one or more races. A 'series' consists of a specified number of races or events.

E1.2 Race Signals
Delete Race Signals. All signals shall be made orally or by other sounds described in this appendix or the sailing instructions.

E1.3 Definitions
(a) Add to the definition *Interested Party*: 'but not a competitor when acting as an observer'.

(b) Delete the definition *Two-Length Zone* and add a new definition, *Four-Length Zone*: 'The area around a *mark* or *obstruction* within a distance of four hull lengths of the boat nearer to it.' Wherever *'two-length zone'* is used in rule 18 replace it with *'four-length zone'*.

E1.4 Personal Buoyancy
Rule 1.2 is changed to 'When on board a rescue boat, each competitor shall be responsible for wearing personal buoyancy adequate for the conditions.'

E1.5 Aerials
Transmitter aerial extremities shall be adequately protected. When a protest committee finds that a competitor has broken this rule it shall either warn him and give him time to comply or penalize him.

E2 PART 2 WHEN BOATS MEET
Rule 21 is changed to
CAPSIZED OR ENTANGLED
If possible, a boat shall avoid a boat that is capsized or

entangled, or has not regained control after capsizing or entanglement. A boat is capsized when her masthead is in the water. Two or more boats are entangled when lying together for a period of time so that no boat is capable of manoeuvring to break free of the other(s).

E3 PART 3 CONDUCT OF A RACE
E3.1 Races with Observers
The race committee may appoint race observers, who may be competitors. They shall remain in the control area while boats are *racing* and they shall hail and repeat the identity of boats that contact a *mark* or another boat. Such hails shall be made from the control area. Observers shall report all unresolved incidents to the race committee at the end of the heat.

E3.2 Course Board
Rule J2.1(4) is deleted. A course board showing the course and the limits of the control area and launching area(s) shall be located next to or within the control area with information clearly visible to competitors while *racing*.

E3.3 Control and Launching Areas
The control and launching area(s) shall be defined by the sailing instructions. Competitors *racing* shall remain in the control area while a heat is in progress, except that competitors may briefly go to and return from the launching area to perform functions permitted in rule E4.5. Competitors not *racing* shall remain outside the control and launching areas except when offering assistance under rule E4.2 or when acting as race observers.

E3.4 Non-applicable Rules
Delete the second sentence of rule 25 and all of rule 33.

E3.5 Starting Races
Rule 26 is changed to
Audible signals for starting a heat shall be at one-minute intervals and shall be a warning signal, a preparatory signal and a starting signal. During the minute before the starting signal, oral signals shall be made at ten-second intervals, and during the final ten seconds at one-second intervals. Each signal shall be timed from the beginning of its sound.

E3.6 Starting Penalties
In rules 29.1 and 30 delete the word 'crew'. Throughout rule 30 oral announcements shall be used instead of flag signals.

E3.7 Starting and Finishing Lines
The starting and finishing lines shall be tangential to, and on the course side of, the starting and finishing *marks*.

E3.8 Individual Recall
In rule 29.1 replace all after 'the race committee shall promptly' with 'twice hail "Recall (sail numbers)"'.

E3.9 General Recall
In rule 29.2 replace all after 'the race committee may' with 'twice hail "General recall" and make two loud sounds'. The warning signal for a new start for the recalled class shall be made shortly thereafter, and the starts for any succeeding classes shall follow the new start.

E3.10 Shortening or Abandoning after the Start
In rule 32.1(b) replace 'foul weather' with 'thunderstorms'. Delete rule 32.1(c).

E4 PART 4 OTHER REQUIREMENTS WHEN RACING
E4.1 Non-applicable Rules
Rules 43, 47, 48, 49, 50, 52 and 54 are deleted.
E4.2 Outside Help
Rule 41 is changed to

(a) A competitor shall not give tactical or strategic advice to a competitor who is *racing*.

(b) A competitor who is *racing* shall not receive outside help except
(1) A boat that has gone ashore or aground outside the launching area, or become entangled with another boat or a mark, may be freed and relaunched only with outside help from a rescue boat crew.
(2) Competitors who are not *racing* and others may give outside help in the launching area as permitted by rule E4.5.

E4.3 Propulsion
Rule 42 is changed so that any reference to body movement is deleted. Rule 42.3(f) is also deleted.

E4.4 Penalties for Breaking Rules of Part 2
Throughout rule 44 the penalty shall be one turn, including one tack and one gybe.

E4.5 Launching and Relaunching
Rule 45 is changed to
(a) A boat scheduled to *race* in a heat may be launched, held on the bank, taken ashore or relaunched at any time during the heat. However, she shall not be released between the preparatory and starting signals.

(b) Boats shall be launched or recovered only from within a launching area, except as provided in rule E4.2(b)(1).

(c) While ashore or within a launching area, boats may be adjusted, drained of water or repaired; have their sails changed or reefed; have entangled objects removed; or have radio equipment repaired or changed.

E4.6 Person in Charge
In rule 46 replace 'have on board' with 'be radio-controlled by'.

E4.7 Radio
(a) A competitor shall not transmit radio signals that cause interference with the radio reception of other boats.

(b) A competitor found to have broken rule E4.7(a) shall not *race* until he has proven compliance with that rule.

E4.8 Boat Out of Radio Control
A competitor who loses radio control of his boat shall promptly hail and repeat '(The boat's sail number) out of control'. Such a boat shall be considered to have retired and shall thereafter be an *obstruction*.

E5 PART 5 PROTESTS, REDRESS, HEARINGS, MISCONDUCT AND APPEALS
E5.1 Right to Protest; Right to Request Redress or Rule 69 Action
Add to rule 60.1(a): 'A *protest* alleging a breach of a rule of Part 2, 3 or 4 shall be made only by a competitor within the control or launching area and by a boat scheduled to *race* in the heat in which the incident occurred.'

E5.2 Informing the Protestee
In rule 61.1(a) replace all after the first sentence with 'When her *protest* concerns an incident in the racing area that she is involved in or sees, she shall twice hail "(Her own sail number) protest (the sail number of the other boat)".'

E5.3 Protest Time Limit
In rule 61.3 replace 'two hours' with '15 minutes' and add: 'A boat intending to protest shall also inform the race committee within five minutes of the end of the relevant heat.'

E5.4 Accepting Responsibility
A boat that acknowledges breaking a rule of Part 2, 3 or 4 before the *protest* is found to be valid may retire from the relevant heat without further penalty.

E5.5 Redress
(a) Add to rule 62.1:

(e) radio interference, or
(f) an entanglement or grounding because of the action of
a boat that was breaking a rule of Part 2 or of a vessel not
racing that was required to keep clear.

(b) In rule 62.2 replace 'two hours' with '15 minutes'.

E5.6 Right to Be Present
In rule 63.3(a) replace 'shall have been on board' with 'shall
have been radio-controlling them'.

E5.7 Taking Evidence and Finding Facts
Add to rule 63.6: 'Evidence about an alleged breach of a rule
of Part 2, 3 or 4 given by competitors shall be accepted only
from a competitor who was within the control or launching
area and whose boat was scheduled to *race* in the heat in
which the incident occurred.'

E5.8 Penalties and Exoneration
When a protest committee finds that a boat has broken rule
E3.3, E4.2(a) or E4.5, it shall either disqualify her from her
next race or require her to make one or more penalty turns in
her next race as soon as possible after *starting*.

E5.9 Decisions on Redress
Add to rule 64.2: 'If a boat given redress was damaged, she
shall be given reasonable time, but not more than 30 minutes,
to effect repairs before her next heat.'

E5.10 Reopening a Hearing
In rule 66 replace '24 hours' with 'ten minutes'.

E6 APPENDIX G IDENTIFICATION ON SAILS
Appendix G is changed as follows:

(a) The text of rule G1.1 before rule G1.1(a) is changed to
Every boat of an ISAF Radio Sailing Division (RSD) class shall
display a sail number on both sides of each sail. Class
insignia and national letters shall be displayed on mainsails
as stated in rules G1.1(a), G1.1(b) and E6(f)(1).

(b) Rule G1.1(c) is changed to
a sail number, which shall be the last two digits of the boat
registration number or the competitor's personal number
allotted by the relevant issuing authority. A single-digit
number shall be prefixed with a '0'. There shall be space in
front of a sail number for the prefix '1', which may be
required by the race committee where there is a conflict
between sail numbers. Where a conflict remains, the race
committee shall require that sail numbers be suitably
changed until the conflict is resolved. Any prefix '1' or other
required change shall become part of the sail number.

(c) Delete the sentence after rule G1.1(c).

(d) Rule G1.2(b) is changed to
The height of characters and distance between them on the
same and opposite sides of the sail shall be as follows:

	Minimum	Maximum
Class insignia:		
Except where positioned back to back, shortest distance between insignia on opposite sides of sail	20 mm	
Sail numbers:		
Height of characters	100 mm	110 mm
Shortest distance between adjoining characters on same side of sail	20 mm	30 mm
Shortest distance between sail numbers on opposite sides of sail and between sail numbers and other identification	60 mm	

National letters:		
Height of characters	60 mm	70 mm
Shortest distance between adjoining characters on same side of sail	13 mm	23 mm
Shortest distance between national letters on opposite sides of sail	40 mm	

(e) Rule G1.3 is changed to
(1) Class insignia may be positioned back to back on
opposite sides of the sail where the design coincides.
Otherwise class insignia, sail numbers and national
letters shall be positioned at different heights, with those
on the starboard side being uppermost.
(2) On a mainsail, sail numbers shall be positioned
above the national letters and below the class insignia.
(3) Sail numbers shall be positioned on a mainsail above
the line perpendicular to the luff through the quarter
leech point.

(f) Where the size of a sail makes it impossible to comply with
the minimum dimensions in rule E6(d) or the positioning
requirements in rule E6(e)(3), exceptions are permitted in
the following order of priority:
(1) omission of national letters;
(2) position of the mainsail sail numbers lower than
the line perpendicular to the luff through the quarter
leech point;
(3) reduction of the shortest distance between sail numbers
on opposite sides of the sail provided the shortest distance
is not less than 20 mm;
(4) reduction of the height of sail numbers.

APPENDIX F
APPEALS PROCEDURES

*See rule 70. A national authority may change this appendix by
prescription but it shall not be changed by sailing instructions.*

F1 APPEALS AND REQUESTS
Appeals, requests by protest committees for confirmation
or correction of their decisions, and requests for
interpretations of the *rules* shall be made to the national
authority of the venue.

F2 SUBMISSION OF DOCUMENTS
F2.1 Within 15 days of receiving the protest committee's
written decision or its decision not to reopen a hearing, the
appellant shall send an appeal and a copy of the protest
committee's decision to the national authority. The appeal
shall state why the appellant believes the protest committee's
decision or its procedures were incorrect.

F2.2 The appellant shall also send, with the appeal or as soon
as possible thereafter, all of the following documents that are
available to her:

(a) the written *protest(s)* or request(s) for redress;

(b) a diagram, prepared or endorsed by the protest
committee, showing the positions and tracks of all boats
involved, the course to the next *mark* and the required side,
the force and direction of the wind, and, if relevant, the
depth of water and direction and speed of any current;

(c) the notice of race, the sailing instructions, any other
conditions governing the event, and any changes to them;

(d) any additional relevant documents; and

(e) the names, postal and e-mail addresses, and telephone
numbers of all *parties* to the hearing and the protest
committee chairman.

F2.3 A request from a protest committee for confirmation or correction of its decision shall be sent within 15 days of the decision and shall include the decision and the documents listed in rule F2.2. A request for an interpretation of the *rules* shall include assumed facts.

F3 RESPONSIBILITIES OF NATIONAL AUTHORITY AND PROTEST COMMITTEE
Upon receipt of an appeal or a request for confirmation or correction, the national authority shall send to the *parties* and protest committee copies of the appeal or request and the protest committee's decision. It shall ask the protest committee for any relevant documents listed in rule F2.2 not sent by the appellant or the protest committee, and the protest committee shall promptly send them to the national authority. When the national authority has received them it shall send copies to the *parties*.

F4 COMMENTS
The *parties* and protest committee may make comments on the appeal or request or on any of the documents listed in rule F2.2 by sending them in writing to the national authority. Comments on any document shall be made within 15 days of receiving it from the national authority. The national authority shall send copies of the comments to the *parties* and protest committee as appropriate.

F5 INADEQUATE FACTS; REOPENING
The national authority shall accept the protest committee's finding of facts except when it decides they are inadequate. In that case it shall require the committee to provide additional facts or other information, or to reopen the hearing and report any new finding of facts, and the committee shall promptly do so.

F6 WITHDRAWING AN APPEAL
An appellant may withdraw an appeal before it is decided by accepting the protest committee's decision.

APPENDIX G
IDENTIFICATION ON SAILS

See rule 77.

G1 ISAF INTERNATIONAL CLASS BOATS
G1.1 Identification
Every boat of an ISAF International Class or Recognized Class shall carry on her mainsail and, as provided in rules G1.3(d) and G1.3(e) for letters and numbers only, on her spinnaker and headsail

(a) the insignia denoting her class;

(b) at all international events, except when the boats are provided to all competitors, national letters denoting her national authority from the table below. For the purposes of this rule, international events are ISAF events, world and continental championships, and events described as international events in their notices of race and sailing instructions; and

(c) a sail number of no more than four digits allotted by her national authority or, when so required by the class rules, by the international class association. The four-digit limitation does not apply to classes whose ISAF membership or recognition took effect before 1 April 1997. Alternatively, if permitted in the class rules, an owner may be allotted a personal sail number by the relevant issuing authority, which may be used on all his boats in that class. Sails measured before 31 March 1999 shall comply with rule G1.1 or with the rules applicable at the time of measurement.

NATIONAL SAIL LETTERS

National authority	Letters	National authority	Letters
Algeria	ALG	American Samoa	ASA
Andorra	AND	Angola	ANG
Antigua	ANT	Argentina	ARG
Australia	AUS	Austria	AUT
Azerbaijan	AZE	Bahamas	BAH
Bahrain	BRN	Barbados	BAR
Belarus	BLR	Belgium	BEL
Bermuda	BER	Brazil	BRA
British Virgin Islands	IVB	Bulgaria	BUL
Canada	CAN	Cayman Islands	CAY
Chile	CHI	China, PR	CHN
Chinese Taipei	TPE	Columbia	COL
Cook Islands	COK	Croatia	CRO
Cuba	CUB	Cyprus	CYP
Czech Republic	CZE	Denmark	DEN
Dominican Republic	DOM	Ecuador	ECU
Egypt	EGY	El Salvador	ESA
Estonia	EST	Fiji	FIJ
Finland	FIN	France	FRA
FYRO Macedonia	MKD	Germany	GER
Great Britain	GBR	Greece	GRE
Grenada	GRN	Guam	GUM
Guatemala	GUA	Hong Kong	HKG
Hungary	HUN	Iceland	ISL
India	IND	Indonesia	INA
Ireland	IRL	Israel	ISR
Italy	ITA	Jamaica	JAM
Japan	JPN	Kazakhstan	KAZ
Kenya	KEN	Korea	KOR
Kuwait	KUW	Latvia	LAT
Lebanon	LIB	Libya	LBA
Liechtenstein	LIE	Lithuania	LTU
Luxembourg	LUX	Malaysia	MAS
Malta	MLT	Mauritius	MRI
Mexico	MEX	Micronesia	FSM
Moldova	MDA	Monaco	MON
Morocco	MAR	Myanmar	MYA
Namibia	NAM	The Netherlands	NED
Netherlands Antilles	AHO	New Zealand	NZL
Norway	NOR	Pakistan	PAK
Papua New Guinea	PNG	Paraguay	PAR
Peru	PER	Philippines	PHI
Poland	POL	Portugal	POR
Puerto Rico	PUR	Qatar	QAT
Romania	ROM	Russia	RUS
Samoa	SAM	San Marino	SMR
Seychelles	SEY	Singapore	SIN
Slovak Republic	SVK	Slovenia	SLO
Solomon Islands	SOL	South Africa	RSA
Spain	ESP	Sri Lanka	SRI
St Lucia	LCA	Sweden	SWE
Switzerland	SUI	Tahiti	TAH
Thailand	THA	Trinidad & Tobago	TRI
Tunisia	TUN	Turkey	TUR
Ukraine	UKR	United Arab Emirates	UAE
United States of America	USA	Uruguay	URU
US Virgin Islands	ISV	Venezuela	VEN
Yugoslavia	YUG	Zimbabwe	ZIM

G1.2 Specifications
(a) National letters and sail numbers shall be in capital letters and Arabic numerals, clearly legible and of the same colour. Commercially available typefaces giving the same or better legibility than Helvetica are acceptable.

(b) The height of characters and space between adjoining characters on the same and opposite sides of the sail shall be related to the boat's overall length as follows:

Overall length	Minimum height	Minimum space between characters and from edge of sail
under 3.5 m	230 mm	45 mm
3.5 m–8.5 m	300 mm	60 mm
8.5 m–11 m	375 mm	75 mm
over 11 m	450 mm	90 mm

G1.3 Positioning

Class insignia, national letters and sail numbers shall be positioned as follows:

(a) Except as provided in rules G1.3(d) and G1.3(e), class insignia, national letters and sail numbers shall when possible be wholly above an arc whose centre is the head point and whose radius is 60% of the leech length. They shall be placed at different heights on the two sides of the sail, those on the starboard side being uppermost.

(b) The class insignia shall be placed above the national letters. If the class insignia is of such a design that two of them coincide when placed back to back on both sides of the sail, they may be so placed.

(c) National letters shall be placed above the sail number.

(d) The national letters and sail number shall be displayed on the front side of a spinnaker but may be placed on both sides. They shall be displayed wholly below an arc whose centre is the head point and whose radius is 40% of the foot median and, when possible, wholly above an arc whose radius is 60% of the foot median.

(e) The national letters and sail number shall be displayed on both sides of a headsail whose clew can extend behind the mast 30% or more of the mainsail foot length. They shall be displayed wholly below an arc whose centre is the head point and whose radius is half the luff length and, if possible, wholly above an arc whose radius is 75% of the luff length.

G2 OTHER BOATS

Other boats shall comply with the rules of their national authority or class association in regard to the allotment, carrying and size of insignia, letters and numbers. Such rules shall, when practicable, conform to the above requirements.

G3 CHARTERED OR LOANED BOATS

When so stated in the notice of race or sailing instructions, a boat chartered or loaned for an event may carry national letters or a sail number in contravention of her class rules.

G4 WARNINGS AND PENALTIES

When a protest committee finds that a boat has broken a rule of this appendix it shall either warn her and give her time to comply or penalize her.

G5 CHANGES BY CLASS RULES

ISAF classes may change the rules of this appendix provided the changes have first been approved by the ISAF.

APPENDIX H
WEIGHING CLOTHING AND EQUIPMENT

See rule 43. This appendix shall not be changed by sailing instructions or prescriptions of national authorities.

H1 Items of clothing and equipment to be weighed shall be arranged on a rack. After being saturated in water the items shall be allowed to drain freely for one minute before being weighed. The rack must allow the items to hang as they would hang from clothes hangers, so as to allow the water to drain freely. Pockets that have drain-holes that cannot be closed shall be empty, but pockets or items that can hold water shall be full.

H2 When the weight recorded exceeds the amount permitted, the competitor may rearrange the items on the rack and the measurer shall again soak and weigh them. This procedure may be repeated a second time if the weight still exceeds the amount permitted.

H3 A competitor wearing a dry-suit may choose an alternative means of weighing the items.

(a) The dry-suit and items of clothing and equipment that are worn outside the dry-suit shall be weighed as described above.

(b) Clothing worn underneath the dry-suit shall be weighed as worn while *racing*, without draining.

(c) The two weights shall be added together.

APPENDIX J
NOTICE OF RACE AND SAILING INSTRUCTIONS

See rules 88.2(a) and 89.2. The term 'race' includes a regatta or other series of races.

J1 NOTICE OF RACE CONTENTS

J1.1 The notice of race shall include the following information:

(1) the title, place and dates of the race and name of the organizing authority;

(2) that the race will be governed by the *rules* as defined in *The Racing Rules of Sailing*;

(3) a list of any other documents that will govern the event (for example, *The Equipment Rules of Sailing*, to the extent that they apply), stating where or how each document or a copy of it may be seen;

(4) the classes to race, any handicap or rating system that will be used and the classes to which it will apply, conditions of entry and any restrictions on entries;

(5) the times of registration and warning signals for the practice race or first race, and succeeding races if known.

J1.2 The notice of race shall include any of the following that would help competitors decide whether to attend the event or that conveys other information they will need before the sailing instructions become available:

(1) identification of any racing rules that will be changed, a summary of the changes, and a statement that the changes will appear in full in the sailing instructions (see rule 86);

(2) that advertising will be restricted to Category A (see ISAF Regulation 20) and other information related to Regulation 20;

(3) that the ISAF Sailor Classification Code will apply;

(4) for an international event, any prescriptions of the national authority that may require advance preparation;

(5) the procedure for advance registration or entry, including fees and any closing dates;

(6) an entry form, to be signed by the boat's owner or owner's representative, containing words such as 'I agree to be bound by *The Racing Rules of Sailing* and by all other *rules* that govern this event';

(7) measurement procedures or requirements for measurement or rating certificates;

(8) the time and place at which the sailing instructions will be available;

(9) any changes to class rules, referring specifically to each rule and stating the change;

(10) the courses to be sailed;

(11) the penalty for breaking a rule of Part 2, other than the Two-Turns Penalty;

(12) denial of the right of appeal, subject to rule 70.4;

(13) the scoring system, if different from the Low Point System in Appendix A, the number of races scheduled and the minimum number that must be completed to constitute a series;

(14) prizes.

J2 SAILING INSTRUCTION CONTENTS
J2.1 The sailing instructions shall include the following information:

(1) that the race will be governed by the *rules* as defined in *The Racing Rules of Sailing*;

(2) a list of any other documents that will govern the event (for example, *The Equipment Rules of Sailing*, to the extent that they apply);

(3) the schedule of races, the classes to race and times of warning signals for each class;

(4) the course(s) to be sailed, or a list of *marks* from which the course will be selected and, if relevant, how courses will be signalled;

(5) descriptions of *marks*, including starting and finishing *marks*, stating the order and side on which each is to be left and identifying all rounding *marks* (see rule 28.1);

(6) descriptions of the starting and finishing lines, class flags and any special signals to be used;

(7) the time limit, if any, for *finishing*;

(8) the handicap or rating system to be used, if any, and the classes to which it will apply;

(9) the scoring system, included by reference to Appendix A, to class rules or other *rules* governing the event, or stated in full. State the number of races scheduled and the minimum number that must be completed to constitute a series.

J2.2 The sailing instructions shall include those of the following that will apply:

(1) that advertising will be restricted to Category A (see ISAF Regulation 20) and other information related to Regulation 20;

(2) that the ISAF Sailor Classification Code will apply;

(3) replacement of the relevant rules of Part 2 with the *International Regulations for Preventing Collisions at Sea* or other government right-of-way rules, the time(s) or place(s) they will apply, and any night signals to be used by the race committee;

(4) changes to the racing rules permitted by rule 86, referring specifically to each rule and stating the change (if rule 86.2 applies, state the authorization);

(5) changes to the prescriptions of the national authority (see rule 87);

(6) at an international event, a copy in English of the prescriptions of the national authority that will apply;

(7) changes to class rules, referring specifically to each rule and stating the change;

(8) restrictions controlling changes to boats when supplied by the organizing authority;

(9) the registration procedure;

(10) measurement or inspection procedure;

(11) location(s) of official notice board(s);

(12) procedure for changing the sailing instructions;

(13) safety requirements, such as requirements and signals for personal buoyancy, check-in at the starting area, and check-out and check-in ashore;

(14) declaration requirements;

(15) signals to be made ashore and location of signal station(s);

(16) the racing area (a chart is recommended);

(17) approximate course length and approximate length of windward legs;

(18) description of any area designated by the race committee to be an *obstruction* (see the definition *Obstruction*);

(19) the time limit, if any, for boats other than the first boat to *finish*;

(20) time allowances;

(21) the location of the starting area and any applicable restrictions;

(22) any special procedures or signals for individual or general recall;

(23) boats identifying *mark* locations;

(24) any special procedures or signals for changing the position of a *mark* after the start;

(25) any special procedures for shortening the course or for *finishing* a shortened course;

(26) restrictions on use of support boats, plastic pools, radios, etc.; on hauling out; and on outside assistance provided to a boat that is not *racing*;

(27) the penalty for breaking a rule of Part 2, other than the Two-Turns Penalty;

(28) penalization without a hearing under rule 67 for breaking rule 42;

(29) whether Appendix P will apply;

(30) protest procedure and times and place of hearings;

(31) if rule N1.4(b) will apply, the time limit for requesting a hearing under that rule;

(32) denial of the right of appeal, subject to rule 70.4;

(33) the national authority's approval of the appointment of an international jury under rule 90(b);

(34) substitution of competitors;

(35) the minimum number of boats appearing in the starting area required for a race to be started;

(36) when and where races *postponed or abandoned* for the day will be resailed;

(37) tides and currents;

(38) prizes;

(39) other commitments of the race committee and obligations of boats.

APPENDIX K
NOTICE OF RACE GUIDE

This guide provides a notice of race designed primarily for major championship regattas for one or more classes. It therefore will be particularly useful for world, continental and national championships and other events of similar importance. It can be downloaded from the ISAF website (www.sailing.org) as a basic text for producing a notice of race for any particular event.
The guide can also be useful for other events. However, for such events some of the paragraphs will be unnecessary or undesirable. Organizing authorities should therefore be careful in making their choices.
This guide relates closely to Appendix L, Sailing Instructions Guide, and its extended version Appendix LE on the ISAF website, the introduction to which contains principles that also apply to a notice of race.
To use this guide, first review rule J1 and decide which paragraphs will be needed. Paragraphs that are required by rule J1.1 are marked with an asterisk (*). Delete all inapplicable or unnecessary paragraphs. Select the version preferred where there is a choice. Follow the directions in the left margin to fill in the spaces where a solid line (_____) appears and select the preferred wording if a choice or option is shown in brackets ([. . .]).
After deleting unused paragraphs, renumber all paragraphs in sequential order. Be sure that paragraph numbers are correct where one paragraph refers to another.
The items listed below, when applicable, should be distributed with the notice of race, but should not be included as numbered paragraphs within the notice.

1 An entry form, to be signed by the boat's owner or owner's representative, containing words such as 'I agree to be bound by The Racing Rules of Sailing *and by all other rules that govern this event.'*
2 In an international event, the applicable prescriptions of the national authority in English.
3 List of sponsors, if appropriate.
4 Lodging and camping information.
5 Description of meal facilities.
6 Race committee and [protest committee] [jury] members.
7 Special mooring or storage requirements.
8 Sail and boat repair facilities and ship's chandlers.
9 Charter boat availability.

On separate lines, insert the full name of the regatta, the inclusive dates from measurement or the practice race until the final race or closing ceremony, the name of the organizing authority, and the city and country.

_____

_____

_____

_____

NOTICE OF RACE

1 RULES

1.1* The regatta will be governed by the rules as defined in The *Racing Rules of Sailing.*

Insert the name. List by number and title the prescriptions that will apply. If the second sentence is used, state the relevant prescriptions in full.

1.2 The following prescriptions of the _____ national authority will apply [and will be stated in full in the sailing instructions]. [Of these, those that may require advance preparation are stated in full below.]

Use only if the national authority for the venue of the event has not adopted a prescription to rule 87.

(OR)
1.2 No national authority prescriptions will apply.

List by name any other documents that govern the event; for example, The Equipment Rules of Sailing, to the extent that they apply.

1.3* _____ will apply.

See rule 86. Insert the rule number(s) and summarize the changes.

1.4 Racing rule(s) _____ will be changed as follows: _____. The changes will appear in full in the sailing instructions.

Inform competitors of proper changes. Insert the rule number(s) and class name. Make a separate statement for the rules of each class.

1.5 Rule(s) _____ of the _____ class rules [will not apply] [is (are) changed as follows: _____].

1.6 If there is a conflict between languages the English text will take precedence.

2 ADVERTISING
Advertising will be restricted to Category A.

See ISAF Regulation 20. Include other applicable information related to Regulation 20.

3* ELIGIBILITY AND ENTRY

Insert the class(es).

3.1 The regatta is open to all boats of the _____ class(es).

(OR)

Insert the class(es) and eligibility requirements.

3.1 The regatta is open to boats of the _____ class(es) that _____.

Insert the postal, fax and e-mail addresses and entry closing date.

3.2 Eligible boats may enter by completing the attached form and sending it, together with the required fee, to _____ by _____.

Insert any conditions.

3.3 Late entries will be accepted under the following conditions: _____.

Insert any restrictions.

3.4 The following restrictions on the number of boats apply: _____.

4 CLASSIFICATION
The ISAF Sailor Classification Code will apply.

5 FEES

Insert all required fees for racing.

5.1 Required fees are as follows:
Class   Fee

_____   _____
_____   _____
_____   _____

Insert optional fees (e.g. for social events).

5.2 Other fees:
_____
_____

Use only when a class is divided into fleets racing a qualifying series and a final series.

6 QUALIFYING SERIES AND FINAL SERIES
The regatta will consist of a qualifying series and a final series.

7 SCHEDULE

Insert the day, date and times.

7.1* Registration:
Day and date _____
From _____   To _____

Insert the day, date and times.

7.2 Measurement and inspection:
Day and date _____
From _____   To _____

Revise as desired and insert the dates and classes. Include a practice race if any. When the series consists of qualifying races and final races, specify them. The schedule can also be given in an attachment.

7.3* Dates of racing:

Date	Class _____	Class _____
_____	racing	racing
_____	racing	reserve day
_____	reserve day	racing
_____	racing	racing
_____	racing	racing

Insert the classes and numbers.

7.4 Number of races:

Class	Number	Races per day
_____	_____	_____
_____	_____	_____

Insert the time.

7.5* The scheduled time of the warning signal for the [practice race] [first race] [each day] is _____.

8 MEASUREMENTS
Each boat shall produce a valid [measurement] [rating] certificate.

(OR)
Each boat shall produce a valid [measurement] [rating] certificate. In addition the following measurements [may] [will] be taken: _____.

List the measurements with appropriate references to the class rules.

Insert the time, date and location.

Insert a number or letter. Provide a marked map with driving instructions.

Insert a number or letter. Provide a marked map or chart.

Include the description.

Insert a number or letter. A method of illustrating various courses is shown in Addendum A of Appendix L or LE. Insert the course length if applicable.

Include paragraph 12.1 only when the Two-Turns Penalty will not be used. Insert the number of places or describe the penalties.

Insert the class(es).

Include only if the protest committee is an international jury or another provision of rule 70.4 applies. Use 'jury' only if referring to an international jury.

Include only if the Low Point System is replaced by the Bonus Point System.

Include only if neither of the Appendix A scoring systems will be used. Describe the system.

Insert the number.

Insert the numbers throughout.

9 SAILING INSTRUCTIONS
The sailing instructions will be available after _____ on _____ at _____.

10 VENUE

10.1 Attachment _____ shows the location of the regatta harbour.

10.2 Attachment _____ shows the location of the racing areas.

11 THE COURSES
The courses to be sailed will be as follows: _____.

(OR)
The diagrams in Attachment _____ show the courses, including the approximate angles between legs, the order in which marks are to be passed, and the side on which each mark is to be left. [The approximate course length will be _____.]

12 PENALTY SYSTEM

12.1 The Scoring Penalty, rule 44.3, will apply. The penalty will be _____ places.

(OR)
12.1 The penalties are as follows: _____.

12.2 For the _____ class(es) rules 44.1 and 44.2 are changed so that only one turn, includ-ing one tack and one gybe, is required.

12.3 Decisions of the [protest committee] [jury] will be final as provided in rule 70.4.

13 SCORING

13.1 The Bonus Point System of Appendix A will apply.

(OR)
13.1 The scoring system is as follows: _____.

13.2 _____ races are required to be completed to constitute a series.

13.3(a) When fewer than _____ races have been completed, a boat's series score will be the total of her race scores.
(b) When from _____ to _____ races

have been completed, a boat's series score will be the total of her race scores excluding her worst score.
(c) When _____ or more races have been completed, a boat's series score will be the total of her race scores excluding her two worst scores.

Insert the identi-fication markings. National letters are suggested for international events.

14 SUPPORT BOATS

Support boats shall be marked with _____.

15 BERTHING

Boats shall be kept in their assigned places in the [boat park] [harbour].

16 HAUL-OUT RESTRICTIONS

Keel boats shall not be hauled out during the regatta except with and according to the terms of prior written permission of the race committee.

17 DIVING EQUIPMENT AND PLASTIC POOLS

Underwater breathing apparatus and plastic pools or their equivalent shall not be used around keel boats between the pre-paratory signal of the first race and the end of the regatta.

Insert any alterna-tive text that applies. Describe the radio communication bands or frequen-cies that will be used or allowed.

18 RADIO COMMUNICATION

A boat shall neither make radio transmissions while racing nor receive radio communications not available to all boats. This restriction also applies to mobile telephones.

When perpetual trophies will be awarded state their complete names.

19 PRIZES

Prizes will be given as follows: _____.

20 DISCLAIMER OF LIABILITY

Competitors participate in the regatta entirely at their own risk. See rule 4, Decision to Race. The organizing authority will not accept any liability for material damage or personal injury or death sustained in conjunction with or prior to, during, or after the regatta.

Insert the currency and amount.

21 INSURANCE

Each participating boat shall be insured with valid third-party liability insurance with a minimum cover of _____ per event or the equivalent.

Insert necessary contact information: person or organization, address, telephone, fax, e-mail.

22 FURTHER INFORMATION

For further information please contact _____.

APPENDIX L
SAILING INSTRUCTIONS GUIDE

This guide provides a set of tested sailing instructions designed primarily for major championship regattas for one or more classes. It therefore will be particularly useful for world, continental and national championships and other events of similar importance. The guide can also be useful for other events; however, for such events some of these instructions will be unnecessary or undesirable. Race officers should therefore be careful in making their choices.

An expanded version of the guide, Appendix LE, is available on the ISAF website (www.sailing.org). It contains provisions applicable to the largest and most complicated multi-class events, as well as variations on several of the sailing instructions recommended in this appendix. It will be revised from time to time, to reflect advances in race management techniques as they develop, and can be downloaded as a basic text for producing the sailing instructions for any particular event. Appendix L can also be downloaded from the ISAF website.

The principles on which all sailing instructions should be based are as follows:

1 They should include only two types of statement: the intentions of the race committee and the obligations of competitors.
2 They should be concerned only with racing. Information about social events, assignment of moorings, etc., should be provided separately.
3 They should not change the racing rules except when clearly desirable.
4 They should not repeat or restate any of the racing rules.
5 They should not repeat themselves.
6 They should be in chronological order; that is, the order in which the competitor will use them.
7 They should, when possible, use words or phrases from the racing rules.

To use this guide, first review rule J2 and decide which instructions will be needed. Instructions that are required by rule J2.1 are marked with an asterisk (*). Delete all inapplicable or unnecessary instructions. Select the version preferred where there is a choice. Follow the directions in the left margin to fill in the spaces where a solid line (_____) appears and select the preferred wording if a choice or option is shown in brackets ([. . .]).

After deleting unused instructions, renumber all instructions in sequential order. Be sure that instruction numbers are correct where one instruction refers to another.

On separate lines, insert the full name of the regatta, the inclusive dates from measurement or the practice race until the final race or closing ceremony, the name of the organizing authority, and the city and country

_____

_____

_____

_____

_____

SAILING INSTRUCTIONS

1 RULES

1.1* The regatta will be governed by the rules as defined in The Racing Rules of Sailing.

Insert the name. State the relevant prescriptions in full.

1.2 The following prescriptions of the _____ national authority will apply: _____.

Use only if the national authority for the venue of the event has not adopted a prescription to rule 87.

(OR)
1.2 No national authority prescriptions will apply.

List by name any other documents that govern the event; for example, The Equipment Rules of Sailing, to the extent that they apply.

1.3* _____ will apply.

See rule 86. Insert the rule number(s) and state the changes.

1.4 Racing rule(s) _____ will be changed as follows: _____.

Insert the rule number(s) and class name. Make a separate statement for the rules of each class.

1.5 Rule(s) _____ of the _____ class rules [will not apply] [is (are) changed as follows: _____].

1.6 If there is a conflict between languages the English text will take precedence.

Insert the location(s).

2 NOTICES TO COMPETITORS
Notices to competitors will be posted on the official notice board(s) located at _____.

3 CHANGES TO SAILING INSTRUCTIONS

Change the times if different.

Any change to the sailing instructions will be posted before 0900 on the day it will take effect, except that any change to the schedule of races will be posted by 2000 on the day before it will take effect.

4 SIGNALS MADE ASHORE

Insert the location.

4.1 Signals made ashore will be displayed at _____.

Insert the number of minutes.

4.2 When flag AP is displayed ashore, '1 minute' is replaced with 'not less than _____ minutes' in the race signal AP.

Insert the number of minutes.

(OR)
4.2 Flag D with a sound means 'The warning signal will be made not less than _____ minutes after flag D is displayed. [Boats are requested not to leave the harbour until this signal is made.]'

Delete if a class rule applies.

4.3 When flag Y is displayed ashore, rule 40.1 applies at all times while afloat. This changes the Part 4 preamble.

5 SCHEDULE OF RACES

Revise as desired and insert the dates and classes. Include a practice race if any. When the series consists of qualifying races and final races, specify them. The schedule can also be given in an attachment.

5.1* Dates of racing:

Date	Class _____	Class _____
_____	racing	racing
_____	racing	reserve day
_____	reserve day	racing
_____	racing	racing
_____	racing	racing

Insert the classes and numbers.

5.2* Number of races:

Class	Number	Races per day
_____	_____	_____
_____	_____	_____

(a) Reserve days may be used if races are not completed as scheduled or if the race committee considers it unlikely that races will be completed as scheduled.
(b) One extra race per day may be sailed, provided that no class becomes more than one race ahead of schedule.

Insert the time.

5.3* The scheduled time of the warning signal for the first race each day is _____.

5.4 When there has been a long postponement and when more than one race (or sequence of races, for two or more classes) will be held on the same day, the warning signal for the first race and each succeeding race will be made as soon as practicable. To alert boats that a race or sequence of races will begin soon, an orange flag will be displayed with one sound for at least four minutes before a warning signal is displayed.

Insert the time.

5.5 On the last day of the regatta no warning signal will be made after _____.

6* CLASS FLAGS

Insert the classes and names or descriptions of the flags.

Class flags will be:

Class	Flag
_____	_____
_____	_____
_____	_____

7 RACING AREAS

Insert a number or letter.

Attachment _____ shows the location of racing areas.

8 THE COURSES

Insert a number or letter. A method of illustrating various courses is shown in Addendum A. Insert the course length if applicable.

8.1* The diagrams in Attachment _____ show the courses, including the approximate angles between legs, the order in which marks are to be passed, and the side on which each mark is to be left. [The approximate course length will be _____.]

8.2 No later than the warning signal, the race committee signal boat will display the approximate compass bearing of the first leg.

8.3 When there is a gate, boats shall sail between the gate marks from the direction of the previous mark and round either gate mark.

8.4 Courses will not be shortened. This changes rule 32.

Include only when changing positions of marks is impracticable.

8.5 Legs of the course will not be changed after the preparatory signal. This changes rule 33.

9 MARKS

Change the mark numbers as needed and insert the descriptions of the marks. Use the second alternative when Marks 4S and 4P form a gate, with Mark 4S to be left to starboard and Mark 4P to port. Unless clear from the course diagrams, state which marks are rounding marks.

9.1* Marks 1, 2, 3 and 4 will be _____.

(OR)
9.1* Marks 1, 2, 3, 4S and 4P will be _____.

Insert the description.

Insert the number of minutes.

Insert the descriptions of the marks.

9.2 New marks, as provided in instruction 12.1, will be _____.

Describe the starting and finishing marks: for example, the race committee signal boat at the starboard end and a buoy at the port end. Instruction 11.2 will describe the starting line and instruction 13 the finishing line.

9.3* The starting and finishing marks will be _____.

Insert the channel number.

9.4 A race committee boat signalling a change of a leg of the course is a mark as provided in instruction 12.2.

10 AREAS THAT ARE OBSTRUCTIONS

Describe each area by its location and any easily recognized details of appearance.

The following areas are designated as obstructions: _____.

11 THE START

Include only if the asterisked option in rule 26 will be used. Insert the number of minutes.

11.1 Races will be started by using rule 26 with the warning signal given _____ minutes before the starting signal.

For large fleets and long starting lines.

(OR)
11.1 Races will be started by using rule 26 with the following addition: An attention signal (flag F with one sound) will be made five minutes before the warning signal for the first class to start. The race committee will designate the course to be sailed before or with the attention signal. Flag F will be removed with one sound one minute before the warning signal. This changes rule 27.1.

Reverse 'port' and 'starboard' when the mark is to be left to starboard.

Describe any starting system other than that stated in rule 26.

(OR)
11.1 Races will be started as follows: _____. This changes rule 26.

11.2* The starting line will be between staffs displaying orange flags on the starting marks.

(OR)
11.2* The starting line will be

Insert the description.

between a staff displaying an orange flag on the starting mark at the starboard end and the port-end starting mark.

(OR)
11.2* The starting line will be _____.

11.3 Boats whose warning signal has not been made shall avoid the starting area.

11.4 A boat starting later than _____ minutes after her starting signal will be scored Did Not Start. This changes rule A4.

11.5 If any part of a boat's hull, crew or equipment is on the course side of the starting line during the two minutes before her starting signal, the race committee will display flag V. It will be displayed until all boats have sailed completely to the pre-start side, but not after the starting signal.

(OR)
11.5 If any part of a boat's hull, crew or equipment is on the course side of the starting line during the two minutes before her starting signal and she is identified, the race committee will attempt to broadcast her sail number on VHF channel _____. Failure to make a broadcast or to time it accurately will not be grounds for a request for redress. This changes rule 62.1(a).

12 CHANGE OF THE NEXT LEG OF THE COURSE

12.1 To change the next leg of the course, the race committee will move the original mark (or the finishing line) to a new position.

(OR)
12.1 To change the next leg of the course, the race committee will lay a new mark (or move the finishing line) and remove the original mark as soon as practicable. When in a subsequent change a new mark is replaced, it will be replaced by an original mark.

12.2 Except at a gate, boats shall pass between the race committee boat signalling the change of the next leg and the nearby mark, leaving the mark to port and the race committee boat to starboard. This changes rule 28.1.

13* THE FINISH

The finishing line will be between staffs displaying orange flags on the finishing marks.

(OR)
The finishing line will be between a staff displaying an orange flag on the finishing mark at the starboard end and the port-end finishing mark.

(OR)
The finishing line will be _____.

14 PENALTY SYSTEM

Include instruction 14.1 only when the Two-Turns Penalty will not be used. Insert the number of places or describe the penalties.

14.1 The Scoring Penalty, rule 44.3, will apply. The penalty will be _____ places.

(OR)
14.1 The penalties are as follows: _____.

Insert the class(es).

14.2 For the _____ class(es) rules 44.1 and 44.2 are changed so that only one turn, including one tack and one gybe, is required.

14.3 A boat that has taken a penalty under rule 31.2 or 44.1 shall complete an acknowledgment form at the race office within the protest time limit.

Here and below, use 'jury' only when referring to an international jury.

14.4 As provided in rule 67, the [protest committee] [jury] may, without a hearing, penalize a boat that has broken rule 42.

(OR)
14.4 Appendix P will apply [as changed by instruction(s)] [14.2] [and] [14.5].

Recommended only for junior events.

14.5 Rule P2.3 will not apply and rule P2.2 is changed so that it will apply to any protest after the first one.

15 TIME LIMITS

Insert the classes and times. Omit the Mark 1 time limit if inapplicable.

15.1* Time limits are as follows:

Class	Time limit	Mark 1 time limit
_____	_____	_____
_____	_____	_____
_____	_____	_____

If no boat has passed Mark 1 within the Mark 1 time limit the race will be abandoned.

Insert the time (or different times for different classes).

15.2 Boats failing to finish within _____ after the first boat sails the course and finishes will be scored Did Not Finish. This changes rules 35 and A4.

16 PROTESTS AND REQUESTS FOR REDRESS

16.1 Protest forms are available at the race office. Protests shall be delivered there within the protest time limit.

Change the time if different.

16.2 For each class, the protest time limit is 90 minutes after the last boat has finished the last race of the day. [The same time limit applies to protests by the race committee and [protest committee] [jury] about inci-dents they observe in the racing area and to requests for redress. This changes rules 61.3 and 62.2.]

Change the posting time if different. Insert the jury room location and the time for the first hearing.

16.3 Notices will be posted within 30 minutes of the protest time limit to inform competitors of hearings in which they are parties or named as witnesses. Hearings will be held in the jury room, located at _____, beginning at _____.

16.4 Notices of protests by the race committee or [protest committee] [jury] will be posted to inform boats under rule 61.1(b).

16.5 A list of boats that, under instruction 14.4, have acknowledged breaking rule 42 or have been disqualified by the [protest committee] [jury] will be posted before the protest time limit.

16.6 Breaches of instructions 11.3, 14.3, 18, 19.2, 22, 23 and 24 will not be grounds for a protest by a boat. This changes rule 60.1(a). Penalties for these breaches may be less than disqualification if the [protest committee] [jury] so decides.

16.7 On the last day of the regatta a request for reopening a hearing shall be delivered
(a) within the protest time limit if the party requesting reopening was informed of the decision on the previous day;
(b) no later than 30 minutes after the party requesting reopening was informed of the decision on that day. This changes rule 66.

Change the time if different.

Include only if the protest committee is an international jury or another provision of rule 70.4 applies.

16.8 Decisions of the [protest committee] [jury] will be final as provided in rule 70.4.

17 SCORING

Include only if the Low Point System is replaced by the Bonus Point System.

17.1* The Bonus Point System of Appendix A will apply.

(OR)

Include only if neither of the Appendix A scoring systems will be used. Describe the system.

17.1* The scoring system is as follows: _____.

Insert the number.

17.2* _____ races are required to be completed to constitute a series.

Insert the numbers throughout.

17.3 (a) When fewer than _____ races have been completed, a boat's series score will be the total of her race scores.
(b) When from _____ to _____ races have been completed, a boat's series score will be the total of her race scores excluding her worst score.
(c) When _____ or more races have been completed, a boat's series score will be the total of her race scores excluding her two worst scores.

18 SAFETY REGULATIONS

18.1 Check-out and check-in: _____.

Insert the procedure for check-out and check-in.

18.2 A boat that retires from a race

shall notify the race committee as soon as possible.

19 REPLACEMENT OF CREW OR EQUIPMENT

19.1 Substitution of competitors will not be allowed without prior written approval of the [race committee] [protest committee] [jury].

19.2 Substitution of damaged or lost equipment will not be allowed unless approved by the race committee. Requests for substitution shall be made to the committee at the first reasonable opportunity.

20 EQUIPMENT AND MEASUREMENT CHECKS

A boat or equipment may be inspected at any time for compliance with the class rules and sailing instructions. On the water, a boat can be instructed by a race committee measurer to proceed immediately to a designated area for inspection.

21 OFFICIAL BOATS

Insert the descriptions. If appropriate, use different identification markings for boats performing different duties.

Official boats will be marked as follows: _____.

22 SUPPORT BOATS

22.1 Team leaders, coaches and other support personnel shall stay outside areas where boats are racing from the time of the preparatory signal for the first class to start until all boats have finished or the race committee signals a postponement, general recall or abandonment.

Insert the identification markings. National letters are suggested for international events.

22.2 Support boats shall be marked with _____.

23 HAUL-OUT RESTRICTIONS

Keel boats shall not be hauled out during the regatta except with and according to the terms of prior written permission of the race committee.

24 DIVING EQUIPMENT AND PLASTIC POOLS

Underwater breathing apparatus and plastic pools or their equivalent shall not be used around keel boats between the preparatory signal of the first race and the end of the regatta.

Insert any alternative text that applies. Describe the radio communication bands or frequencies that will be used or allowed.

25 RADIO COMMUNICATION

A boat shall neither make radio transmissions while racing nor receive radio communications not available to all boats. This restriction also applies to mobile telephones.

26 PRIZES

If perpetual trophies will be awarded state their complete names.

Prizes will be given as follows: _____.

27 DISCLAIMER OF LIABILITY

Competitors participate in the regatta entirely at their own risk. See rule 4, Decision to Race. The organizing authority will not accept any liability for material damage or personal injury or death sustained in conjunction with or prior to, during, or after the regatta.

28 INSURANCE

Insert the currency and amount.

Each participating boat shall be insured with valid third-party liability insurance with a minimum cover of _____ per event or the equivalent.

ADDENDUM A ILLUSTRATING THE COURSE

Shown here are diagrams of course shapes. Any course can be similarly shown. When there is more than one course, prepare a separate diagram for each course and state how each will be signalled.

A Windward-Leeward Course
Start – 1 – 2 – 1 – 2 – Finish

Options for this course include (1) increasing or decreasing the number of laps, (2) deleting the final windward leg, (3) using a gate instead of a leeward mark, (4) using an offset mark at the windward mark, and (5) using the leeward and windward marks as starting and finishing marks.

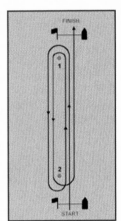

A Windward-Leeward-Triangle Course
Start – 1 – 2 – 3 – 1 – 3 – Finish

Options for this course include (1) increasing or decreasing the number of laps, (2) deleting the last windward leg, (3) varying the interior angles of the triangle (45°–90°–45° and 60°–60°–60° are common), (4) using a gate instead of a leeward mark for downwind legs (but not reaches), (5) using an offset mark at the beginning of downwind legs (but not reaches), and (6) using the leeward and windward marks as starting and finishing marks. Be sure to specify the interior angle at each mark.

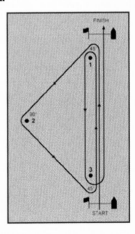

Trapezoid Courses
1. Start – 1 – 2 – 3 – 2 – 3 – Finish
2. Start – 1 – 4 – 1 – 2 – 3 – Finish

Options for these courses include
(1) adding additional legs,
(2) using gates instead of leeward marks for downwind legs
(but not reaches),
(3) varying the interior angles of the reaching legs,
(4) using an offset mark at the beginning of downwind legs (but
not reaches), and
(5) finishing boats upwind rather than on a reach.
Be sure to specify the interior angle of each reaching leg. It is
recommended that Mark 4 be different from the starting mark.

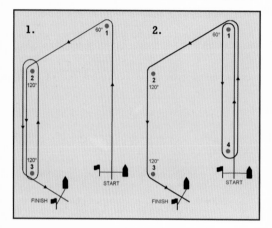

ADDENDUM B
BOATS PROVIDED BY THE
ORGANIZING AUTHORITY

The following sailing instruction is recommended when all
boats will be provided by the organizing authority. It can
be changed to suit the circumstances. When used, it should
be inserted after instruction 3.

4 BOATS

4.1 Boats will be provided for all competitors, who shall
not modify them or cause them to be modified in any way
except that

(a) a compass may be tied or taped to the hull or spars;

(b) wind indicators, including yarn or thread, may be
tied or taped anywhere on the boat;

(c) hulls, centreboards and rudders may be cleaned, but
only with water;

(d) adhesive tape may be used anywhere above the
water line; and

(e) all fittings or equipment designed to be adjusted may
be adjusted, provided that the class rules are complied
with.

4.2 All equipment provided with the boat for sailing
purposes shall be in the boat while afloat.

4.3 The penalty for not complying with one of the above
instructions will be disqualification from all races sailed
in which the instruction was broken.

4.4 Competitors shall report any damage or loss of
equipment, however slight, to the organizing authority's
representative immediately after securing the boat
ashore. The penalty for breaking this instruction, unless
the [protest committee] [jury] is satisfied that the
competitor made a determined effort to comply, will be
disqualification from the race most recently sailed.

4.5 Class rules requiring competitors to be members of
the class association will not apply.

APPENDIX M
RECOMMENDATIONS FOR
PROTEST COMMITTEES

This appendix is advisory only; in some circumstances
changing these procedures may be advisable. It is
addressed primarily to protest committee chairmen but
may also help judges, jury secretaries, race committees
and others connected with protest and redress hearings.

In a protest or redress hearing, the protest committee
should weigh all testimony with equal care; should
recognize that honest testimony can vary, and even
be in conflict, as a result of different observations and
recollections; should resolve such differences as best
it can; should recognize that no boat or competitor is
guilty until a breach of a *rule* has been established to
the satisfaction of the protest committee; and should
keep an open mind until all the evidence has been heard
as to whether a boat or competitor has broken a *rule*.

M1 PRELIMINARIES (may be performed by race
office staff)
* Receive the *protest* or request for redress.
* Note on the form the time the *protest* or request
  is delivered and the protest time limit.
* Inform each *party*, and the race committee when
  necessary, when and where the hearing will be held.

M2 BEFORE THE HEARING
Make sure that
* each *party* has a copy of or the opportunity to read the
  protest or request for redress and has had reasonable
  time to prepare for the hearing.
* no member of the protest committee is an *interested
  party*. Ask the *parties* whether they object to any
  member. When redress is requested under rule
  62.1(a), a member of the race committee should not
  be a member of the protest committee.
* only one person from each boat (or *party*) is present
  unless an interpreter is needed.
* all boats and people involved are present. If they are
  not, however, the committee may proceed under rule
  63.3(b).
* boats' representatives were on board when required
  (rule 63.3(a)). When the *parties* were in different races,
  both organizing authorities must accept the
  composition of the protest committee (rule 63.8). In a
  measurement *protest* obtain the current class rules and
  identify the authority responsible for interpreting them
  (rule 64.3(b)).

M3 THE HEARING
M3.1 Check the validity of the *protest* or request for
redress.
* Are the contents adequate (rule 61.2 or 62.1)?
* Was it delivered in time? If not, is there good reason
  to extend the time limit (rule 61.3 or 62.2)?
* When required, was the protestor involved in or a
  witness to the incident (rule 60.1(a))?
* When necessary, was 'Protest' hailed and, if required,
  a red flag displayed correctly (rule 61.1(a))?

- When the flag and hail were not necessary was the protestee informed?
- Decide whether the *protest* or request for redress is valid (rule 63.5).
- Once the validity of the *protest* or request has been determined, do not let the subject be introduced again unless truly new evidence is available.

M3.2 Take the evidence (rule 63.6).
- Ask the protestor and then the protestee to tell their stories. Then allow them to question one another. In a redress matter, ask the *party* to state the request.
- Invite questions from protest committee members.
- Make sure you know what facts each *party* is alleging before calling any witnesses. Their stories may be different.
- Allow anyone, including a boat's crew, to give evidence. It is the *party* who normally decides which witnesses to call, although the protest committee may also call witnesses (rule 63.6). The question asked by a *party* 'Would you like to hear N?' is best answered by 'It is your choice.'
- Call each *party's* witnesses (and the protest committee's if any) one by one. Limit *parties* to questioning the witness(es) (they may wander into general statements).
- Invite the protestee to question the protestor's witness first (and vice versa). This prevents the protestor from leading his witness from the beginning.
- Allow a member of the protest committee who saw the incident to give evidence (rule 63.6) but only in the presence of the *parties*. The member may be questioned and may remain in the room (rule 63.3(a)).
- Try to prevent leading questions or hearsay evidence, but if that is impossible discount the evidence so obtained.
- Accept written evidence from a witness who is not available to be questioned only if all *parties* agree. In doing so they forego their rights to question that witness (rule 63.6).
- Ask one member of the committee to note down evidence, particularly times, distances, speeds, etc.
- Invite first the protestor and then the protestee to make a final statement of her case, particularly on any application or interpretation of the *rules*.

M3.3 Find the facts (rule 63.6).
- Write down the facts; resolve doubts one way or the other.
- Call back *parties* for more questions if necessary.
- When appropriate, draw a diagram of the incident using the facts you have found.

M3.4 Decide the *protest* or request for redress (rule 64).
- Base the decision on the facts found (if you cannot, find some more facts).
- In redress cases, make sure that no further evidence is needed from boats that will be affected by the decision

.
M3.5 Inform the parties (rule 65).
- Recall the parties and read them the facts found, conclusions and *rules* that apply, and the decision. When time presses it is permissible to read the decision and give the details later.
- Give any *party* a copy of the decision on request. File the *protest* or request for redress with the committee records.

M4 REOPENING A HEARING (rule 66)
When a *party*, within the time limit, has asked for a hearing to be reopened, hear the *party* making the request, look at any video, etc., and decide whether there is any material new evidence that might lead you to change your decision. Decide whether your

interpretation of the *rules* may have been wrong; be open-minded as to whether you have made a mistake. If none of these applies refuse to reopen; otherwise schedule a hearing.

M5 GROSS MISCONDUCT (rule 69)
M5.1 An action under this rule is not a *protest*, but the protest committee gives its allegations in writing to the competitor before the hearing. The hearing is conducted under the same rules as other hearings but the protest committee must have at least three members (rule 69.1(b)). Use the greatest care to protect the competitor's rights.

M5.2 A competitor or a boat cannot protest under rule 69, but the protest form of a competitor who tries to do so may be accepted as a report to the protest committee, which can then decide whether or not to call a hearing.

M5.3 When it is desirable to call a hearing under rule 69 as a result of a Part 2 incident, it is important to hear any boat-vs.-boat *protest* in the normal way, deciding which boat, if any, broke which *rule*, before proceeding against the competitor under this rule.

M5.4 Although action under rule 69 is taken against a competitor, not a boat, a boat may also be penalized (rule 69.1(b)).

M5.5 The protest committee may warn the competitor (rule 69.1(b)), in which case no report is to be made to national authorities (rule 69.1(c)). When a penalty is imposed and a report is made to national authorities, it may be helpful to recommend whether or not further action should be taken.

M6 APPEALS (rule 70 and Appendix F)
When decisions can be appealed,
- retain the papers relevant to the hearing so that the information can easily be used for an appeal. Is there a diagram endorsed or prepared by the protest committee? Are the facts found sufficient? (Example: Was there an *overlap*? Yes or No. 'Perhaps' is not a fact found.) Are the names of the protest committee members and other important information on the form?
- comments by the protest committee on any appeal should enable the appeals committee to picture the whole incident clearly; the appeals committee knows nothing about the situation.

M7 PHOTOGRAPHIC EVIDENCE
Photographs and videotapes can sometimes provide useful evidence but protest committees should recognize their limitations and note the following points:
- The *party* producing the photographic evidence is responsible for arranging the viewing.
- View the tape several times to extract all the information from it.
- The depth perception of any single-lens camera is very poor; with a telephoto lens it is non-existent. When the camera views two *overlapped* boats at right angles to their course, it is impossible to assess the distance between them. When the camera views them head on, it is impossible to see whether an *overlap* exists unless it is substantial.
- Ask the following questions:
  - Where was the camera in relation to the boats?
  - Was the camera's platform moving? If so in what direction and how fast?
  - Is the angle changing as the boats approach the critical point? Fast panning causes radical change.
  - Did the camera have an unrestricted view throughout?

APPENDIX N
INTERNATIONAL JURIES

See rules 70.4 and 90(b). This appendix shall not be changed by sailing instructions or prescriptions of national authorities.

N1 COMPOSITION, APPOINTMENT AND ORGANIZATION
N1.1 An international jury shall be composed of experienced sailors with excellent knowledge of the racing rules and extensive protest committee experience. It shall be independent of and have no members from the race committee, and be appointed by the organizing authority, subject to approval by the national authority if required (see rule 90(b)), or by the ISAF under rule 88.2(b).

N1.2 The jury shall consist of a chairman, a vice chairman if desired, and other members for a total of at least five. A majority shall be International Judges. The jury may appoint a secretary, who shall not be a member of the jury.

N1.3 No more than two members (three, in Groups M, N and Q) shall be from the same national authority.

N1.4 (a) A jury of ten or more members may divide itself into two or more panels of at least five members each, of which the majority shall be International Judges. If this is done, the requirements for membership of a full jury shall apply to each panel but not to the jury as a whole.
(b)   A jury of fewer than ten members may divide itself into two or three panels of at least three members each, of which the majority shall be International Judges. Members of each panel shall be from at least three different national authorities except in Groups M, N and Q, where they shall be from at least two different national authorities. If dissatisfied with a panel's decision, a *party* is entitled to a hearing by a jury composed in compliance with rules N1.1, N1.2 and N1.3, except concerning the facts found, if requested within the time limit specified in the sailing instructions.

N1.5 When a full jury has fewer than five members, because of illness or emergency, and no qualified replacements are available, it remains properly constituted if it consists of at least three members. At least two members shall be International Judges. When there are three or four members they shall be from at least three different national authorities except in Groups M, N and Q, where they shall be from at least two different national authorities.

N1.6 When the national authority's approval is required for the appointment of an international jury (see rule 90(b)), notice of its approval shall be included in the sailing instructions or be posted on the official notice board.

N1.7 If the jury acts while not properly constituted, the jury's decisions may be appealed.

N2 RESPONSIBILITIES
N2.1 An international jury is responsible for hearing and deciding all *protests*, requests for redress and other matters arising under the rules of Part 5. When asked by the organizing authority or the race committee, it shall advise and assist them on any matter directly affecting the fairness of the competition.

N2.2 Unless the organizing authority directs otherwise, the jury shall
(a) decide questions of eligibility, measurement or boat certificates; and
(b) authorize the substitution of competitors, boats, sails or equipment.

N2.3 If so directed by the organizing authority, the jury shall
(a) make or approve changes to the sailing instructions,
(b) supervise or direct the race committee in the conduct of the races, and
(c) decide on other matters referred to it by the organizing authority.

N3 PROCEDURES
N3.1 Decisions of the jury shall be made by a simple majority vote of all members. When there is an equal division of votes cast, the chairman of the meeting may cast an additional vote.

N3.2 When it is considered desirable that some members not participate in discussing and deciding a *protest* or request for redress, and no qualified replacements are available, the jury remains properly constituted if at least three members remain. At least two members shall be International Judges.

N3.3 Members shall not be regarded as *interested parties* (see rule 63.4) by reason of their nationality.

N3.4 If a panel fails to agree on a decision it may adjourn and refer the matter to the full jury.

APPENDIX P
IMMEDIATE PENALTIES FOR BREAKING RULE 42

This appendix applies only if the sailing instructions so state.

P1 PROTESTS
A member of the protest committee or its designated observer who sees a boat breaking rule 42 may protest her by, as soon as reasonably possible, making a sound signal, pointing a yellow flag at her and hailing her sail number, even if she is no longer *racing*. A boat so protested is not subject to another *protest* under rule 42 for the same incident.

P2 PENALTIES
P2.1 First Protest
When a boat is first protested under rule P1 she may acknowledge her breach by taking a Two-Turns Penalty under rule 44.2. If she fails to do so she shall be disqualified without a hearing.

P2.2 Second Protest
When a boat is protested a second time during the series she may acknowledge her breach by immediately retiring from the race. If she fails to do so she shall be disqualified without a hearing and her score shall not be excluded.

P2.3 Third Protest
When a boat is protested a third time during the series she may acknowledge her breach by immediately retiring from the race and from all other races in the series. If she fails to do so she shall be disqualified without a hearing from all races in the series, with no score excluded, and the protest committee shall consider calling a hearing under rule 69.1(a).

P3 POSTPONEMENT, GENERAL RECALL OR ABANDONMENT
If a boat has been protested under rule P1 and the race committee signals a *postponement*, general recall or *abandonment*, the penalty from her first or second *protest* is cancelled, but the *protest* is counted to determine the number of times she has been protested during the series.

INDEX

You rely on us.
Can we rely on you?

Become an Offshore member from just £4.50 per month.

Last year, our volunteers saved over 7,000 people. But we couldn't have saved a single one of them without the support of people like you. Join Offshore today, and you'll be helping to run the Lifeboat service whose volunteers will be on hand, should you ever get into difficulty at sea.

Call **0800 543210** today.

Or visit **www.rnli.org.uk**

Offshore

FOS2004 registered charity no. 209603

DEFINITIONS

A term used as stated below is shown in italic type or, in preambles, in bold italic type.

Abandon A race that a race committee or protest committee *abandons* is void but may be resailed.

Clear Astern and Clear Ahead; Overlap One boat is *clear astern* of another when her hull and equipment in normal position are behind a line abeam from the aftermost point of the other boat's hull and equipment in normal position. The other boat is *clear ahead*. They *overlap* when neither is *clear astern*. However, they also *overlap* when a boat between them *overlaps* both. These terms do not apply to boats on opposite *tacks* unless rule 18 applies.

Finish A boat *finishes* when any part of her hull, or crew or equipment in normal position, crosses the finishing line in the direction of the course from the last *mark*, either for the first time or after taking a penalty under rule 31.2 or 44.2 or, under rule 28.1, after correcting an error made at the finishing line.

Interested Party A person who may gain or lose as a result of a protest committee's decision, or who has a close personal interest in the decision.

Keep Clear One boat *keeps clear* of another if the other can sail her course with no need to take avoiding action and, when the boats are *overlapped* on the same *tack*, if the *leeward* boat can change course in both directions without immediately making contact with the *windward* boat.

Leeward and Windward A boat's *leeward* side is the side that is or, when she is head to wind, was away from the wind. However, when sailing by the lee or directly downwind, her *leeward* side is the side on which her mainsail lies. The other side is her *windward* side. When two boats on the same *tack* *overlap*, the one on the *leeward* side of the other is the *leeward* boat. The other is the *windward* boat.

Mark An object the sailing instructions require a boat to leave on a specified side, and a race committee boat surrounded by navigable water from which the starting or finishing line extends. An anchor line and objects attached temporarily or accidentally to a *mark* are not part of it.

Obstruction An object that a boat could not pass without changing course substantially, if she were sailing directly towards it and one of her hull lengths from it. An object that can be safely passed on only one side and an area so designated by the sailing instructions are also *obstructions*. However, a boat *racing* is not an *obstruction* to other boats unless they are required to *keep clear* of her, give her *room* or, if rule 21 applies, avoid her.

Overlap See **Clear Astern and Clear Ahead; Overlap.**

Party A *party* to a hearing: a protestor; a protestee; a boat requesting redress; a boat or a competitor that may be penalized under rule 69.1; a race committee or an organizing authority in a hearing under rule 62.1(a).

Postpone A *postponed* race is delayed before its scheduled start but may be started or *abandoned* later.

Proper Course A course a boat would sail to *finish* as soon as possible in the absence of the other boats referred to in the rule using the term. A boat has no *proper course* before her starting signal.

Protest An allegation made under rule 61.2 by a boat, a race committee or a protest committee that a boat has broken a *rule*.

Racing A boat is *racing* from her preparatory signal until she *finishes* and clears the finishing line and *marks* or retires, or until the race committee signals a general recall, *postponement* or *abandonment*.

Room The space a boat needs in the existing conditions while manoeuvring promptly in a seamanlike way.

Rule (a) The rules in this book, including the Definitions, Race Signals, Introduction, preambles and the rules of relevant appendices, but not titles;
(b) ISAF Regulation 19, Eligibility Code; Regulation 20, Advertising Code; and Regulation 21, Anti-Doping Code;
(c) the prescriptions of the national authority, unless they are changed by the sailing instructions in compliance with the national authority's prescription, if any, to rule 87;
(d) the class rules (for a boat racing under a handicap or rating system, the rules of that system are 'class rules');
(e) the notice of race;
(f) the sailing instructions; and
(g) any other documents that govern the event.

Start A boat *starts* when, having been entirely on the pre-start side of the starting line at or after her starting signal, and having complied with rule 30.1 if it applies, any part of her hull, crew or equipment crosses the starting line in the direction of the first *mark*.

Tack, Starboard or Port A boat is on the *tack*, *starboard* or *port*, corresponding to her *windward* side.

Two-Length Zone The area around a *mark* or *obstruction* within a distance of two hull lengths of the boat nearer to it.

Windward See **Leeward and Windward.**

RACE SIGNALS

The meanings of visual and sound signals are stated below. An arrow pointing up or down (▲ ▼) means that a visual signal is displayed or removed. A dot (•) means a sound; five short dashes (- - - - -) mean repetitive sounds; a long dash (–) means a long sound.

Postponement Signals

▲ • • ▼ •

AP Races not started are *postponed*. The warning signal will be made 1 minute after removal unless at that time the race is *postponed* again or *abandoned*.

▲ • •

AP over H Races not started are *postponed*. Further signals ashore.

▲ • •

AP over A Races not started are *postponed*. No more racing today.

Penant 1 ▲ • • ▼ •

Penant 2 ▲ • • ▼ •

Penant 3 ▲ • • ▼ •

Penant 4 ▲ • • ▼ •

Penant 5 ▲ • • ▼ •

Penant 6 ▲ • • ▼ •

A-P over a numeral pennant 1-6 *Postponement* of 1-6 hours from the scheduled startig time

Abandonment Signals

▲ • • • ▼ •

N All races that have started are *abandoned*. Return to the starting area. The warning signal will be made 1 minute after removal unless at that time the race is *abandoned* again or *postponed*.

▲ • • •

N over H All races are *abandoned*. Further signals ashore.

▲ • • •

N over A All races are *abandoned*. No more racing today.

Recall Signals

▲ •

X Individual recall.

▲ • • ▼ •

First Substitute General recall. The warning signal will be made 1 minute after removal.

Preparatory Signals

▲ • ▼ –

P Preparatory signal.

▲ • ▼ –

I Rule 30.1 is in effect.

▲ • ▼ –

Z Rule 30.2 is in effect.

▲ • ▼ –

Black flag. Rule 30.3 is in effect.

Course Change Signals

▲ • •

S The course has been shortened. Rule 32.2 is in effect.

- - - - -

C The position of the next *mark* has been changed

Other Signals

▲ •

L Ashore: A notice to competitors has been posted. Afloat: Come within hail or follow this boat.

- - - - -

M The object displaying this signal replaces a missing *mark*.

▲ •

Y Wear personal buoyancy.

(no sound)

Blue flag or shape. This race committee boat is in position at the finishing line.